241 REAL-WORLD BRAIN TEASERS.

Guided problem-solving in Inventions, Nature, Uncommon Trivia, and Business Innovation.

Invent and Discover

ISBN 979-8775182007 (Amazon.com, hardback)

ISBN 979-8768873325 (Amazon.com, paperback)

ISBN 978-1668599938 (Barnes & Noble, paperback)

ISBN 978-1716146640 (Lulu Press, paperback)

CONTENTS

PART III
EXTRA CHALLENGING PROBLEMS

BONUS - DON'T FORGET YOUR FREE EBOOKS.

Included with the purchase of this book are:

- More brain-teaser problems, with media materials. Download an illustrated ebook.
- SCAMPER - Techniques and tips for developing brainstorm-thinking strategy. How to use problems from this book for training. Download an ebook.
- Access to members-only content and offers via our social groups

Have your FREE copies sent to your inbox:

http://bonus.inventanddiscover.com

INTRODUCTION

In today's world, information about anything and everything under the sun is right at your fingertips. With a simple web search and a couple of clicks, anyone can find facts on practically any subject.

But, when it comes to achieving success in school, at work, or in business, *knowledge* is just half the battle. Look at people who are at the top of their game. What do they have in common? What sets them apart? What are they exceptionally good at?

Thinking out of the box.

Regardless of field or industry, brilliant minds all have the amazing capability to approach problems creatively and find innovative — sometimes unexpected — solutions. In this modern age of easy access to facts and figures, lateral thinking has become especially valuable. It's not so much about *what* you know, but *how* you process this and how you think.

The great news is that anyone can practice and develop these skills!

In this book, you'll find 241 unique, intriguing problems specially designed to flex those mental muscles and train your brain. While the questions revolve mainly around science, technology, and business, we guarantee that these don't just test what you already know. Instead, these exercises are structured in a way that will challenge you to figure things out yourself — no trivia knowledge required.

Each problem gives you a chance to either walk in someone else's shoes as they invent, innovate, or discover solutions to real-life challenges, or devise your own ideas to existing problems in the modern world. Carefully-constructed hints guide you along on the journey, making for an excellent way to train your thought process. In time, this will hopefully make it easier for you to see and *seize* more opportunities in everyday life as well.

WHAT SETS THIS BOOK APART?

Trivia games and quizzes can be interesting but are often pretty straightforward — you either know the answer, or you don't! On the other hand, riddles and logic puzzles can be fun and challenging to solve but don't really enrich nor expand your knowledge much.

Here, you get the best of both worlds. Each quick question leads you through an exciting journey of solving an actual real-world problem by understanding not just the "what" but the "how" and "why" as well.

No matter what age or stage in your life you are, brain teasers can be incredibly beneficial. In children, building lateral thinking from an early age makes all the difference, not just academically but preparing for later life experiences as well. In the elderly, these exercises have been proven to be crucial for maintaining brain health and cognitive function.

Whether you're looking for a fun mental workout to stretch those thinking muscles, sharpen logical reasoning, and practice lateral thinking, or are simply eager to learn some interesting new things, this book can be an excellent companion.

There are no age restrictions nor cultural context requirements to be able to solve and enjoy the challenges in this book — this is for *anyone* who loves learning about the world.

These questions go beyond trivia that is often constrained by what you already know versus what you don't, as well as abstract puzzles that don't really teach you anything concrete. Instead, these enrich your mind with a deeper understanding of how things work, from nature and science to inventions, business, and many more fascinating topics.

By working through real-world problems that other people have faced in various places, contexts, cultures, or times, you can train your brain and hone your thinking skills, effectively preparing yourself to be able to take on any challenges of your own.

HOW YOU CAN USE THIS BOOK

PLAY SOLO

Get your daily mental workout in — challenge yourself with a problem or two every day! Simply work your way through the book from start to finish, choose questions according to chapters arranged by topic and difficulty, or even just pick problems at random.

Don't worry about getting it correct every time or right off the bat. Helpful hints are provided to give you another shot at figuring out the solution, taking you halfway there. And, even if sometimes you still don't quite arrive at the right answer, that's alright, too! The process of generating ideas, analyzing each of these critically, and developing the most promising one towards a solution is a great way to train your brain. How can you go wrong when you're stretching those thinking muscles and learning about the world while you're at it?

WITH A PARTNER OR GROUP

The fun of a trivia or quiz night often depends on the crowd — sometimes, generational gaps and differences in the background can be tricky, making the game considerably less enjoyable.

That's why this book is fantastic for playing with family and friends! Not only do we guarantee that the topics are all kid-friendly and safe-for-work, but everything you need to solve the challenge will also be right in the question and hint. Regardless of age, profession, culture... Everyone can get in on the excitement of brainstorming and bouncing out-of-the-box ideas off each other to get to an answer.

Whether you face off with a partner, organize a team tournament, or arrange a co-op mission to solve problems as a group, you're in for a seriously entertaining (and brain-challenging!) time together.

AS A JUMP-OFF POINT

The brainteasers in this book are an excellent gateway for further learning, spanning various topics around invention, innovation, nature, technology, discovery, and so many other fascinating facets of the world.

Each question's answer comes with an additional tidbit of interesting info, going beyond just your usual nice-to-know trivia. These are meant to give you insight into what makes people tick and how things work and hopefully pique your curiosity to learn more on your own.

Intriguing, entertaining, and thought-provoking, these real-world-scenario brainteasers also make for unique conversation starters with friends and colleagues.

IN THE WORKPLACE

Logical reasoning, analytical problem solving, lateral thinking, and creativity are all extremely important in the workplace, and these brainteasers can be useful tools in evaluating and developing these skills in people.

Human resource practitioners may want to use these questions as part of the process of testing job applicants or candidates for promotion. These can also be used for team-building events, professional development activities, and ideation training.

HOW TO NAVIGATE THIS BOOK

To guide you along, the problems are categorized into three difficulty levels: Easy, Intermediate, and Extra Challenging. Each level is also organized by topic, giving you even more control of what you want to work on and how you want to play.

You *could* choose to work through the problems at random by turning to just any page. However, to truly maximize your experience, we recommend going sequentially from beginning to end.

We also understand how annoying it can be to jump between separate sections to get from question to answer then back again for the next question. That's why we've optimized each format — print, ebook, and audiobook — for your convenience and enjoyment. Read on for more on how to navigate each version.

PAPER BOOK

Questions are found mainly on the right-hand side of each spread, followed immediately by their respective hints at the bottom of the page. Turning the page, you'll find the answers and additional information on the flip side, which would then be at the left-hand side of the spread.

We've designed the book with your ultimate convenience in mind. Unlike with other puzzle or brain teaser books, our easy-to-navigate format means you don't have to skip back and forth between the questions and the end of the book for answers. Once you've worked through the problems on a page, you can turn to the next side for answers.

If and whenever you open up the book at a random spot in the middle, make sure you look only at the right-hand page! That way, you avoid seeing answers to other questions without meaning to.

Solutions, Explanations, and Further Information	**Problems**
	Hints
(See the back of this page for Problems and Hints)	(See the back of this page for Solutions)

EBOOK

The parts of each problem — question, hint, answer with explanation — are separated by page breaks.

Just like the print version, the ebook is formatted specifically for convenient navigation — no jumping back and forth between separate question and answer sections necessary. Just be careful not to scroll or tap ahead to the next page before you're ready!

AUDIOBOOK

The audiobook is a great way to play hands-free or as a group during long drives. To enjoy the book in this format, pausing the playback is highly recommended! Get the most out of each problem by pausing right after the question and before the hint, then again just before the answer. We've also added short sound signals at these points as a helpful reminder for when to pause.

There are built-in breaks in the recording, but as these are just a couple of seconds long, you might want to hit pause yourself to ensure everyone has enough time to discuss and brainstorm.

❧ I ❧
EASY PROBLEMS

BUSINESS INNOVATIONS

1. Baseball is perhaps the quintessential American sport. It's not just the game, but the entire experience—the fanfare, fun, and food. In 1901, Harry Stevens was an entrepreneur who made a living selling ice cream in stadiums. On an abnormally cold April day though, he introduced a new product to crowds to boost his sales. Stevens later maintained his claim on being the inventor of the handheld way of eating this—something that has stood the test of time and is popular to this day. What is this?

HINTS:

1. The cold weather made him decide to sell something hot, but anything too hot would burn people's hands. So, he came up with a convenient way to hold a particular food.

ANSWERS:

1A. He came up with the idea of putting a sizzling sausage in a bun—a hotdog.

Stevens knew that he needed something other than ice cream to keep his business going in cold weather—something hot yet still convenient to snack on at the game. That's why he started selling hot sausages scrved in a split bun 'holder.' Today, hotdogs are still an all-American favorite at sporting events.

QUESTIONS:

2. To conserve forests, the Chinese government imposed additional taxes on products made of wood. Their list of taxable products included some everyday household items - which wooden item topped the list?

3. Manufacturers of mezcal, Mexico's national alcoholic beverage, follow an unusual practice. In each exported bottle, they add a 'guzana' - the caterpillar of a Bombyx agavis butterfly. Why would the manufacturers have started this practice?

4. In the latter half of the 19th century, Swedish engineer Gustaf de Laval invented a reliable and efficient machine to make glass bottles. Despite his rotating mold machines' efficacy and the mass production of bottles it allowed, the enterprise was soon forced to close. Why could such an enterprise have failed?

.   .   .

5. Handing out flyers in the street is a common advertising tactic worldwide. In nearly any urban city, you'll often find people trying to get passers-by to take a leaflet or small brochure. Pedestrians, however, often either ignore them entirely or accept the handout only to throw it away immediately. In the hot summer of 2018, a creative ad agency in Japan came up with a way to get people to accept and hold onto these flyers. In what novel form did they create their clients' brochures?

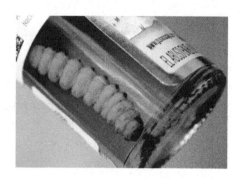

HINTS:

2. *These products are also occasionally found in kitchens elsewhere, though we don't use them as often as the eastern folks do.*

3. *Can adding a Bombyx agavis caterpillar prove the authenticity of an exported product? If so, how?*

4. *The answer lies in mass production. What can the result on the market be?*

5. *The hot weather was the key*

ANSWERS:

2A. Chopsticks.

With China's population of 1.4 billion, regular use of chopsticks has a sizeable impact on the forests. The government is encouraging its people to switch to reusable or non-wooden chopsticks.

3A. The Bombyx agavis is found only in Mexico, and exported bottle that has a caterpillar can be deemed authentic.

The Bombyx agavis is endemic to Mexico, which means it is found only here and nowhere else in the world. Producers of mezcal in another country that may try to falsely market their product as Mexican would not find the Bombyx agavis caterpillar. Thereby, manufacturers of mezcal can establish authenticity.

4A. With mass-produced bottles, the enterprise became unprofitable, and therefore, unviable.

Laval's equipment was so effective that the market was soon flooded with glass bottles. As per the supply-demand law in economics, the prices of the bottles dropped, the margins decreased, and the company was unable to meet its production expenses. The enterprise was forced to close.

5A. Paper fans

By creating something useful out of the flyers, the agency solved the problem of these getting thrown away. Not only were people more willing to take and keep these, but they also became more likely to read the printed info while using these to fan themselves on a hot summer day.

6. With the rise of modern technology, electronic waste (or e-waste) has become a severe environmental issue. In 2010, an international organization found a new use for gold and silver from discarded computer circuits and monitors. What were these precious metals used for?

7. Recreational cruises are known for having amazing amenities on board their giant ocean liners—guests can enjoy everything from movies and musical shows to sports! Specifically for shipboard golf courses, certain companies began to produce golf balls made of special material. What material is used for these unique golf balls?

8. Several years ago, an unusual coffee machine was installed at the Johannesburg airport in South Africa. The device was equipped with a sensor that could read people's faces and sometimes dispense free coffee. In what instances would a machine dispense free coffee?

HINTS:

6. *The prominent organization would require amounts of gold and silver not just once but every few years.*

7. *When playing golf on a ship, it isn't uncommon for balls to be hit overboard and into the water. Wouldn't eco-friendly balls be a great idea?*

8. *Coffee is perfect for perking up your mood and waking you up. What unconscious, spontaneous action makes it obvious that you need a cup of coffee?*

ANSWERS:

6A. Olympic gold and silver medals

During the 2010 Vancouver Winter Olympics, gold and silver from end-of-life electronics were recovered and recycled into athletes' medals. Japan followed suit in 2020 for the Tokyo Olympics.

7A. Compressed fish food

In the (frankly quite likely) event that the golf ball ends up in the ocean, it dissolves into food for sea creatures instead of polluting the waters.

8A. When it detects a passer-by has yawned.

The sensor on the coffee machine uses facial recognition to detect when a person in front of it yawned - an involuntary reaction to fatigue or boredom. The coffee company Douwe Egberts used this as a marketing gimmick and programmed the machine to dispense a free coffee if anyone yawned in front of it. What better way to wake someone up?

9. In Matsushiro, Japan, some hotels have introduced unusual discounts for their guests. If an indicator has a reading of 3, guests receive a free glass of wine; if it is 4 - their room rent will be reduced by 50%; with 5 or higher, their entire stay is complimentary. What does the indicator keep track of?

10. Businesses often incorporate innovative ideas to signal the quality of their products to prospective buyers. One device often includes a set of diatom shells - remnants of primitive, unicellular algae bearing symmetrical patterns in their quality control kit. What scientific device is this?

HINTS:

9. *The indicator is a globally used system that helps monitor what tourists fear most in Japan.*

10. *Diatoms are unicellular algae - one-cell organisms - that lie in transparent, ornate silica-walled houses. What kind of a scientific device would use tiny creatures to establish quality?*

ANSWERS:

9A. Earthquake intensity.

In the event of an earthquake, a hotel in Matsushiro, Japan offers discounts to their guests based on the Richter scale readings of earthquake intensity.

10A. A microscope.

When buying a microscope, the slides with beautiful diatoms offers potential buyers the chance to look at the intricate patterns of the shells and ensure that there are no distortions or imperfections in the image produced by the device.

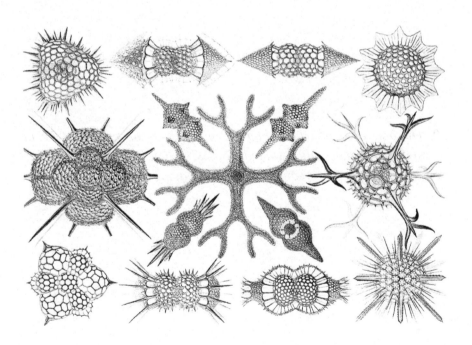

2

CULTURE & ARTS

11. In 18th century Paris, opera was one of the most popular forms of entertainment, especially among the bourgeois. In 1781, one of the esteemed theaters of the Palais-Royal (or Royal Palace) was razed to the ground in a huge fire. Architect Lenoir le Romain quickly built a new theater, putting extensive safety measures in place. However, Parisians were not only still traumatized from the previous disaster but also doubtful of the speed at which the building was reconstructed. Despite all the precautions Lenoir had taken, people were hesitant to attend the opera at the new venue. How did King Louis XVI attract audiences to the inaugural performance?

HINTS:

11. *What is almost always a surefire way to get any customer's attention and interest?*

ANSWERS:

11A. With a free performance

To demonstrate the new theater's safety and stability, the King encouraged people to experience it firsthand. He announced a free opera which successfully drew an audience of around 6,000.

QUESTIONS:

12. Renowned today for its luxury and excellent location right in the city center, Grand Hotel de Milan also boasts of rich history in culture and the arts. One of its most prolific patrons was composer Giuseppe Verdi who lived at the hotel for many years. For the duration of Verdi's residence, the hotel owner ordered that the street in front of the building be covered with straw. What was the reason behind this request?

13. In Beijing, artist Wang Renzheng once roamed the streets for 100 days, collecting material with a vacuum cleaner. However, he was not vacuuming the roads or pavements. He has yet managed to hoover up enough material to later commission bricks to be made of it as an artistic statement. What statement was the artist trying to make?

14. Every writer has their own quirky habits to ensure productivity. On one occasion, the French writer, Victor Hugo, was eager to complete a particular, daunting writing task. What little trick did he use, to discourage himself from socializing for several weeks, in order to complete his writing in time?

.   .   .

15. The Royal Palace in Seoul, South Korea, has an unusual flooring - tiles are set unevenly and have jagged edges. What did the architects hope to achieve with this unconventional design?

HINTS:

12. *The owner wanted to create the very best conditions for his valued, distinguished guest.*

13. *What could take 100 days to hoover up if it wasn't the streets or the pavements? What statement would the bricks make?*

14. *Victor Hugo, as many French men in that era, was usually very conscientious about his looks and spent a lot of time grooming. How did the scissors serve to help him avoid getting derailed from the writing task at hand?*

15. *The architects were instructed to incorporate a design that allowed commoners to show respect to the crown. How did the uneven flooring help?*

ANSWERS:

12A. To keep the noise from the street from disturbing the composer.

Being located along a busy street, the Grand Hotel de Milan was prone to the racket of passing carriages. Covering the streets with straw dampened these sounds and minimized the noise, helping create a more conducive environment for Giuseppi Verdi to compose music.

13A. The artist made a statement against Beijing's terrible air pollution.

Over 100 days, the vacuum cleaner hoovered up the dust and dirt from Beijing's lower atmosphere - which forms the layer of air that the citizens breathe in. The artist commissioned the dust and dirt to be made into bricks as a statement against the severe air pollution.

14A. Hugo gave himself an ugly haircut.

Grooming is often undertaken to keep social appearances. With an ugly haircut, Victor Hugo knew that he could avoid the temptation to socialize and focus on his writing instead. Wonder which classic was the result of such a hair-larious trick?

15A. Walking on uneven tiles, one tends to bend one's head down to navigate the space and avoid tripping, thereby involuntarily showing courtesy and respect to the palace and the king.

The architecture of the Royal Palace in Seoul uses the confusing, complicated patterning of the floor to force people to bow their heads for their own safety while eliciting respect.

3

CUSTOMS & TRADITIONS

16. There's an anecdote about the first lie detector used in the Middle East in ancient times. A priest claimed to have a magic donkey that could catch a liar. The donkey was placed in a dark room, and its tail was smeared with ash. The suspect was led into the dark room to deliver his testimony while holding onto the donkey's tail. The priest claimed that if someone were lying, the donkey would speak in a human voice, whereas the donkey would remain silent if he were honest. How could this odd practice have actually led to the cunning priest discovering the truth?

HINTS:

16. *The suspect was not told that the donkey's tail would be smeared with ash. How would the dark room and the donkey with a dirty tail have been helpful for detecting lies?*

ANSWERS:

16A. Upon exiting the dark room, the priest would know the liars by their clean hands and the honest by ash-smeared hands.

The 'lie detector' assumed that a liar would be too scared to hold onto the tail of the donkey, believing it to be 'magical'. Thereby, an honest person would have no inhibitions in holding the donkey's tail, whereas the liars would. The crafty priest could then identify the liars.

QUESTIONS:

17. Early pilgrims, and even the first North American colonists, carried shells with them on long journeys. Apart from being a talisman for good luck, the shells also served a more practical, prosaic purpose - what was it?

18. In the 5th and 6th centuries, Indian temple priests packed the hollow stems of plants either with sulfur powder or scented resins. This resulted in the sticks burning slowly, releasing brightly colored flames: those filled with sulfur powder gave off a foul smell, whereas those with resins emitted a sweet scent. What have such slow-burning, flame-bursting sticks evolved into since?

19. In Far East Russia lies the Kamchatka peninsula, stretching between the Pacific Ocean, the Bering Sea, and the Sea of Okhotsk. The people who inhabit the Kamchatka peninsula or the Kamchadals used to worship a god called Tuela. They also believed in an ancient myth: if fleas bother the dog of the god Tuela, it results in a particular natural phenomenon. What phenomenon is this?

. . .

HINTS:

17. *Think about the shape and size of a shell; what could you use it for when traveling?*

18. *These days, these sticks are used for festive or special occasions due to the brightly colored flames that erupt from them.*

19. *What is a dog prone to doing when bothered by fleas?*

ANSWERS:

17A. Shells could be used as spoons.

Shells make for handy spoons - an essential when traveling light across distances.

18A. Sparklers - also known as Bengal sparklers.

The temple priests who started using sparkling sticks lived in Bengal, in eastern India, hence the name Bengal sparklers, or sparklers. Sparklers are used as fireworks worldwide.

19A. An earthquake.

The Kamchadals believed that earthquakes are caused when fleas attack the god Tuela's dog. In a bid to get rid of them, the dog starts scratching and shaking himself, resulting in an earthquake. Understandably, such a curious earthquake myth began in Kamchatka - as it is a seismically active zone located along the Pacific Rim. There are more than 300 volcanoes on the Kamchatka peninsula, including 29 active ones, and earthquakes are also extremely frequent.

❦ 4 ❦
FOLK WISDOM

20. The African steppe is challenging terrain. The Bushmen tribes living in the steppes have found a solution to one of their problems: catch a baboon, feed it salt, and then release it. What problem can this solve?

HINTS:

20. *What would the effect of eating too much salt be, especially in the dry steppes?*

ANSWERS:

20A. Locating a source of water.

Wild animals have better-developed senses to locate water and food, as well as sense danger. After being fed salt, the baboon would be thirsty and would likely search for water. By following the thirsty baboon, the Bushmen can also locate a water source. Traveling through difficult terrain, one could look to the animals around for cues on how to survive.

☙ 5 ❧
HISTORICAL HAPPENINGS

21. On December 5, 1951, the city of New York announced an air raid drill for its citizens. The townspeople were instructed to listen for the sound of the siren and immediately run to the nearby shelters. However, a reasonable exception was made for some citizens who were exempted from the training. Apart from hospital patients who might not be able to rush to shelters, which other category of people were exempt from following the drill?

HINTS:

21. *The other exempt group was not indisposed like the hospital patients. Still, if they followed the drill and rushed off to the shelters, it would have affected the commercial interests of certain establishments in the city.*

ANSWERS:

21A. Restaurant visitors.

When the mayor of New York issued the air raid drill notice, restaurant patrons were exempt to ensure that they paid the bill, as they were unlikely to return to do so afterward.

QUESTIONS:

22. During the Vietnam War, anti-aircraft missile systems were an important part of Vietnam's defense. Each of these anti-aircraft crews was assigned a unique key player: one plant grower. Why was the plant grower a crucial member of the crew?

23. In the 18th century, the road from St. Petersburg to Moscow, Russia's two largest cities, was one of the most important thoroughfares in the country. To protect this road, the government was forced to send soldiers to cut down forests surrounding it. What particular problem were they trying to solve?

24. General Julius Caesar is historically renowned for transforming ancient Rome from a republic to an empire through not just his political prowess, but of course, his military mastery as well. He once ordered his soldiers' shields and weapons to be decorated with precious stones and jewels. This was his tactical solution to a certain phenomenon in the army at the time. Why did he do it?

25. Sometimes, criminal ingenuity can be quite incredible. As a key part of their process of creating certain objects, a group of delinquents

in 19th century France were known to run the fruits of their labor through a pile of dust with a broom. What criminal activity were they involved in?

HINTS:

22. *Vietnamese air defense systems' positions were some of the main targets of the United States Air Force.*

23. *In the absence of trees, it became much more difficult for anyone to hide by the road.*

24. *Roman soldiers sometimes felt that their movement was compromised by the weight of their weapons and shields.*

25. *The intention was to give their creations an old, worn-out look*

ANSWERS:

22A. They were in charge of camouflaging the positions of the Vietnamese anti-aircraft missile systems.

These plant experts cultivated vegetation, such as thick, fast-growing bamboo to cover the anti-aircraft missile systems, hiding their position from American Air Forces.

23A. Robbery

The St. Petersburg-Moscow corridor was one of Russia's primary trade routes in the 18th century, making it a hotspot for robbery. The government curbed this problem by ordering the surrounding forests to be cut down—robbers could no longer execute their modus of hiding behind the trees along the road.

24A. To stop soldiers from discarding their weapons on the battlefield.

When fleeing from the battlefield, retreating Roman troops were known to throw down their weapons in order to run faster. This was a great loss to the Roman government, as it not only cost resources to create new weapons, but it was also tantamount to basically handing over arms to the enemy! With Caesar's solution, soldiers became less likely to abandon their weapons—who would want to leave precious jewels behind?

25A. Counterfeiting money

Crisp new bills would be more likely to draw attention and reveal their scheme. Wrinkling and roughing up the fake money would help it blend in with real used bills.

❧ 6 ❧
HOW'D THEY DO IT?

26. If you've ever seen pictures of the traditional Venetian gondolas - the boats that ferry people across the floating city, you'd remark that the gondoliers or boatsmen have just a single paddle and seem to only paddle on one side. Sailing any craft often requires two paddles or oars, or a single oar alternating between both sides to keep the boat balanced - yet what allows the gondolas to follow a straight line with only a single, one-sided paddle?

HINTS:

26. *The gondoliers do not alternate the paddle on both sides; they only paddle along the right side of the boat. What feature on the boat could compensate for this asymmetry?*

ANSWERS:

26A. An asymmetrical hull

To offset the single paddle, gondolas have an asymmetrical hull, which allows the gondoliers to paddle only on the right or starboard side, follow a straight line, and not run in circles in place. This gives the gondolas their distinct list - they seem more immersed to the right side than the left.

QUESTIONS:

27. In the north European country of Estonia, a draft law has proposed a new punishment system for speed limit offenders. If someone exceeds the speed limit by over 40 kilometers per hour, a monetary fine is enforced. For smaller violations, the driver is given the option of another punishment, enforced immediately by the apprehending police officer. How is the violator punished?

28. In 1998, the Prime Minister of Bhutan - the small mountainous country in Southeast Asia, introduced the concept of "Gross National Happiness" as a paradigm for alternate development. This concept is deeply rooted in their culture. In the mid-20th century, a revolutionary invention believed to adversely impact happiness levels was banned across the country. What invention was this?

29. Yachtsman and traveler Trevor Robertson spent a whole year in one of the world's coldest regions: Antarctica. According to him, one of the most challenging things in those conditions was reading books because thin pages would often freeze together. How did Trevor Robinson deal with frozen pages while reading?

. . .

30. France has long been known as the capital of fine arts. To nurture promising talents, art education in the country was free in the 19th century. However, the Paris School of Fine Arts didn't have the capacity to accept each and every applicant. To avoid having to take in international students without being accused of being stingy, what did the school begin to require?

HINTS:

27. *Most speed violations occur to save time in transit. Estonia's new punishment deters such time-saving behavior quite effectively.*

28. *What 20th-century invention spreads bad news that can dampen levels of happiness?*

29. *He used what was immediately and readily available to him to generate heat.*

30. *This would give local applicants higher chances of getting in compared to foreigners.*

ANSWERS:

27A. A waiting period is enforced upon the violator before he can resume driving.

To discourage drivers from speeding to save time, Estonia's punishment enforces a 45 minute waiting period for violations of up to 20 kilometers per hour or an hour for those between 20-40 kilometers per hour. The waiting period means drivers are required to stand by the side of the road and are unable to drive, hence deterring those who wish to save time.

28A. The television.

As global news networks expanded, Bhutanese citizens often heard negative news on their television sets. The authorities banned television in the country for many years. On June 2, 1999, the ban was lifted, and the first broadcast in many years announced the silver jubilee of Jigme Singye Wangchuck - a former king of Bhutan.

29A. Robertson used the heat from his hands to thaw the book's pages.

As he read one page of the book, Robertson would place his palm on the next, allowing his body heat to warm it and get it ready for turning.

30A. A French language proficiency test

To prioritize local talent and avoid paying tuition for those from abroad, the Department of Fine Arts began to include a French language test as one of the entrance requirements. This exam was, of course, much easier to pass for local native speakers than for foreigners.

31. In northern Europe, cold weather often makes it dangerous for pedestrians to walk through the city streets. Iceland has mitigated this problem with the help of its numerous hot springs. What innovative idea have the authorities rolled out to ensure safer roads for pedestrians and drivers?

32. In the 1970s, the keepers at the Moscow Zoo were faced with a difficult task: how to move large crocodiles from the winter terrarium to the summer one? Ideally, the crocodiles need to be tied during transportation, but how do you tie up such massive beasts? The staff changed certain conditions in the winter terrarium to help them effectively tie up the crocodiles - what did they do?

HINTS:

31. *Cold weather causes ice to form on roads and sidewalks, making navigation difficult. How can hot water springs help?*

32. *Crocodiles are cold-blooded creatures. How did the staff use that trait to tie up the massive crocodiles?*

ANSWERS:

31A. Heated sidewalks and streets.

With so many underground springs, it was possible to pipe the hot water to flow under roads and sidewalks to heat the surface. This helps roads and sidewalks remain above freezing temperature and prevents ice formation without spending additional energy. Thus, Iceland has created heated streets that ensure ice-free navigation for citizens.

32A. They turned off the heating in the winter terrarium, the reptiles became sluggish and went into hibernation, and the staff was able to tie them up for transport.

Reptiles spend most of their time sunning themselves, as their cold-blooded systems need more heat to run effectively. By lowering the temperatures in the winter terrarium, zoo staff ensured that the reptiles would go into hibernation and cease movement and were able to tie and transport them more easily.

HUMAN BEHAVIOR

33. American industrialist Henry Ford known for his pioneering system of assembly lines in factories employed a strange payment system for a team of specialists under one of his enterprises: they were paid not for their working hours, but for their leisure time. The specialists were hired to repair a conveyor belt, yet why were they paid for their leisure time instead of working hours?

HINTS:

33. *Henry Ford's tactic was aimed at the efficiency of his enterprise. How would workers strive to speed up their work time, and lengthen their rest hours?*

ANSWERS:

33A. To ensure that the conveyor is repaired swiftly and effectively, to run with as few stops as possible, to ensure more leisure hours.

The team of specialists spent their time in a comfortable room where they could relax, except when a red light signal went off - indicating that the conveyor had broken down. The team had to rush to the workshop, repair the conveyor belt, and could then return to their leisure. The payment scheme ensured that the better the repairs, the more rest time they would have, and the better their pay.

QUESTIONS:

34. Some airlines provide passengers who would like to sleep on board, a choice between two sleep masks. What would influence the passenger's choice of mask?

35. In Germany, some nursing homes for the aged have non-functioning, or fake bus stops nearby - they look like actual bus stops, but no buses run through them. What purpose could such bus stops serve?

36. Back in the days of long sailing voyages, scurvy, an illness caused by a lack of vitamin C, was a real scourge for sailors out at sea. To prevent this in his crew as they sailed around the world, British naval captain James Cook ordered aboard barrels of sauerkraut, a cabbage dish rich in vitamin C. However, he soon resolved for it to be served primarily in the officers' mess deck. What was the reason behind the need for officers to somewhat conspicuously consume sauerkraut?

· · ·

37. The hotel management at a large property in Johannesburg once fired a cleaner on the grounds that he was "mentally challenged". They stated that he had been given a simple cleaning task, over which he spent 4 days! When asked, the cleaner exclaimed, "There are 40 of them, two on each floor". Despite that, he was fired. What task was he allocated, that caused his statement to seal his fate?

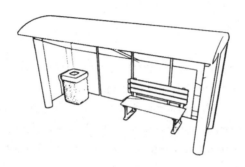

HINTS:

34. *Apart from blocking the light out, could the sleep masks serve another purpose? To inform the crew of something, perhaps?*

35. *The stops are periodically monitored by hospital staff, why would they need to do so?*

36. *Captain Cook found that English sailors were not accustomed to— and as a result, put off by—the taste of sauerkraut.*

37. *The cleaner's statement indicates that the building is a tall one, and the task was perhaps misunderstood.*

ANSWERS:

34A. If they prefer to dine onboard or not allows them to choose between two sleep masks.

One mask says: do not disturb. The other says: wake up during lunch. The passenger can choose masks based on whether he/she wants to dine on board or would prefer to sleep it off.

35A. To ensure patients with Alzheimer's disease or dementia do not wander too far from the nursing homes.

Patients with Alzheimer's disease or dementia have impaired memory. The nursing homes create an illusion of a bus stop outside, and the patients often choose to sit down in wait for a bus to take them to the desired destination. By regularly monitoring these bus stops, caregivers can lead the patients back before they wander away. In recent years, this practice is under ethical consideration, and the pros and cons are still being weighed.

36A. The officers were used to serve as an example for the other sailors.

James Cook wanted his crew to overcome their unfamiliarity and objections and just consume the sauerkraut. By showing the sailors that the senior officers were enjoying the dish, he eventually got them to eat it as well.

37A. To wash elevators.

The janitor had not only misunderstood the task, but he had also spent 4 days, washing the same elevators on every floor of the hotel building!

❧ 8 ❧

I WONDER WHY...?

38. The daily routine in military units is often regulated by sound alarms. In one instance, an Australian training unit in the outbacks introduced a trumpet-like alarm in their barracks. However, their alarm system ran into unexpected problems and had to be changed to a different kind of alarm. The reason? The birds in the outback! How could the birds have forced a change in the alarm systems?

HINTS:

38. *The birds seemed to cause a disruption in the alarm sounds issued for military command. The alarm had to merely be changed from the trumpet-like sound to another sound.*

ANSWERS:

38A. Lyrebirds were mimicking the sound of the alarm and issuing 'false alarms' of their own.

The Australian outback is inhabited by the superb lyrebird which is an excellent mimic, known to faithfully reproduce even the sound of the human voice and car reverse horns. When the birds mimicked the trumpet-like sound, the routine of the military unit was frequently disrupted. Hence the alarms had to be changed from the trumpet-like sound to one that was more challenging for the birds.

QUESTIONS:

39. At a military school, during an exam, a teacher walked in, sat down, and began tapping his table with the pencil. Shortly after that, one student stood up, walked over to the teacher, and was awarded an A grade without a word being exchanged or an exam sheet being handed in. What could have caused such a peculiar outcome?

40. Khari Baoli in New Delhi, India, is Asia's largest wholesale market. The vendors and some locals seem to be quite at ease as they wander through the market in search of what they want, yet foreign tourists are prone to bouts of sneezes and coughs upon entering the market. What strange reason could be causing this?

41. In the 1930s, Soviet Union stadiums in some cities had two poles erected off the field. Each pole had a different color of balloons tied to them - for instance, one pole would have three red balloons, whereas the other had two blue balloons. The number of balloons on each pole

changed throughout the game. What purpose did the colored balloons serve?

42. At the end of the 19th century, the Russian city of Vitebsk saw its first power plant. To instill a sense of curiosity, the facility charged a small fee for the public to visit and watch the power plant at work. After the visit, imagine the puzzlement of many townspeople who seemed to run late for other appointments they had. What could be the reason for their untimeliness?

HINTS:

39. *The clue lies in the tapping, which perhaps, the student had listened to carefully.*

40. *The bouts of sneezing and coughing are set off by some of the market's products - what could be sold at the market to induce such reaction in foreign tourists?*

41. *These stadiums often hosted soccer games, what could the fans be most interested in?*

42. *Think of what helped run the first power plants, and how that energy source could tamper with other devices?*

ANSWERS:

39A. The teacher had tapped out a message in Morse code, requesting students to approach him for a grade and skip writing the exam.

Morse code is used to exchange messages via a series of dots and dashes, or short and long signals - a technique often used by military regiments. As this exam was about communication, the student who picked up on the teacher's seemingly random behavior, and decoded the message, was able to achieve a good grade. The others who hadn't mastered Morse code were left to plod on with the lengthy exam.

40A. Spices.

Among other products like dry fruits, rice, and tea, Khari Baoli also sells various spices. The heady mix of powdered and whole spices in the market can set off a tickle in the nose in those unaccustomed to it.

41A. The scores of the soccer teams.

In the 1930s, not every stadium in the Soviet Union had score-boards. The balloons on the poles served to indicate the score of each team, and the balloon colors matched the team colors. This would be so much more difficult if these were basketball courts.

42A. Magnetized pocket watches and wristwatches.

Since the 19th century, most power plants have operated on dynamos - an electrical generator that creates a direct current with the help of a powerful magnet. The electrical charges in the power plant would have magnetized the metallic watches, and disrupted their time-keeping abilities, causing the factory visitors to run late. A visit to the facility then was often followed by one to the watch repairmen.

43. In one of the posher hotels in New York, an employee has one specialized duty: she is stationed on the hotel rooftop when it is sunny and oversees guests who are sunbathing there. What duty does she perform for the sunbathing hotel guests?

44. During 1991, US military operation, 'Desert Storm' launched against the Iraqi dictator, Saddam Hussein, each army unit was equipped with a chicken coop. Each coop had a White Leghorn chicken, and like most fowl, these are sensitive creatures. What role did the chickens play in the military operation?

45. In the 1970s, an unusual chessboard was made with pieces that fitted into special grooves to hold their place. While magnets were often used for chessboards, in this particular circumstance, they were deemed too dangerous for the game. Where was this game being played?

HINTS:

43. *What is the greatest danger when sunbathing? Her duty involves 20-minute cycles - what does she do?*

44. *Most fowl have better-developed senses of smell than humans. How could this be used to military advantage?*

45. *Magnets may disrupt precise electronic devices. Yet it was crucial to have chess pieces that were held in place - where was the game happening?*

. . .

ANSWERS:

43A. Reminds guests to turn over when sunbathing.

To prevent sunburn and undesirable tan marks, this employee was responsible for reminding clients to turn over and ensure an even tan.

44A. To detect and defend from chemical attacks.

The Iraqi offensive was well-known for its use of chemical attacks, namely tabun and mustard gas. The cooped chickens would sense the chemical gases quicker than humans, panic and asphyxiate, much like a canary in the coal mine, which would serve as a warning for the military units.

45A. At a space station.

In the 1970s, the Mission Control Center played a game against the astronauts on the space station. With a lot of precise electronic equipment onboard, the space station was equipped with a specially-designed grooved chessboard rather than a magnetic one.

❧ 9 ❧

INGENIOUS INVENTIONS

46. In the 1930s, an American store manager was watching a customer and his child - the latter was dragging a toy at the end of a rope. Inspired, he invented something for his store that could allow customers to buy more goods, and voila, it worked. What was his invention commonly seen in supermarkets around the world?

HINTS:

46. *The customer's child had a toy car at the end of a rope. He was dragging it along as his father made the purchase, and the store owner realized how it could be repurposed to ensure customers bought more.*

ANSWERS:

46A. A shopping cart.

The customer had conveniently placed his stack of purchases on the toy car, and everything was being pulled along by the child. The store owner realized that 'specialty carts' could allow customers to check out more items, and thereby increase sales.

QUESTIONS:

47. One can find all kinds of unusual things on the internet - such as wedding rings embedded with a GPS navigator, bearing a small display screen with numbers. What would numbers on such wedding rings signify?

48. Concerned about the health and hygiene of his daughter, American businessman Puneet Nanda sparked some innovation into an everyday object. He added an electric light that would turn off in exactly two minutes and managed to make her daily routine a little more interesting. What device did he innovate upon?

49. Sweden has long been encouraging its citizens to adopt an active and environment-friendly lifestyle. For their safety, a remarkable invention was introduced recently - a neck collar with a high compression gas container and acceleration sensors. What is this device for?

50. With the rise of smartphones, payphone booths have become entirely unnecessary, and most cities are clearing them off their streets. However, recently, London authorities decided not to dismantle their

famous red telephone booths and have instead installed solar panels on the roofs and retooled and repainted them green. What can these refurbished booths now be used for?

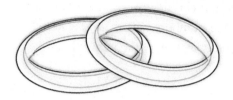

HINTS:

47. *The numbers can and will change over time, yet the display screens on both rings will always show the same number.*

48. *What is part of a young child's daily routine that should optimally last two minutes?*

49. *In what circumstances would the high compression gas chamber be triggered? It takes 0.1 seconds to effect a rapid change in the size and shape of the neck collar. Who might need it?*

50. *What use could the solar panels serve? Could people still use these booths for communication?*

ANSWERS:

47A. The distance between lovers.

The GPS sensors detect how far apart the two wedding rings are from one another and can determine the distance between the bearers, or lovers. Hence the numbers will change when the lovers move apart, but both rings will always show the same figures.

48A. A toothbrush.

Lighting up a toothbrush made brushing more enjoyable for the young girl, and the two-minute glow served as a reminder of just how long and thorough she needed to be.

49A. In case of a biking accident, the inflatable collar can expand to protect the cyclist's head and neck.

If the cyclist experiences a sharp jolt, the collar instantly inflates into a helmet-like airbag that can protect the head and neck from impact.

50A. To charge the mobile devices.

The rise of smartphones also means we are more in need of charging stations while on the move. London's refurbished telephone booths, with their rooftop solar panels, allow anyone to charge their mobile phones. The booths are supported by advertising revenue and still help keep people in touch.

51. Scientists in Japan are developing new technology that will allow houses to be floated off the ground, balanced on magnetic cushions - much like the technology behind the magnetic levitating trains, Maglev. What adversity could these houses prove effective in?

52. Diabetic patients rely on the constant monitoring of their blood glucose levels which is often done by frequent extractions of blood. In the USA, scientists are developing an innovative, non-invasive device to monitor the glucose content of tears. In what object could such a device be installed for the convenience of diabetic patients?

53. The years between World War 1 and World War 2 saw a rapid rise in military technology. In the early 1920s, inventors came up with a new way to practice air combat techniques safely. During these training sessions, several aircraft would engage in mock combat, equipped with a particular device in place of machine guns. This device would then help determine the winner afterward. What was it?

HINTS:

51. *How would temporarily lifting houses off the ground help? What are Japan's citizens most wary of?*

52. *If the device will monitor glucose levels in tear fluid, it would need to be as close to the tear gland as possible.*

53. *Pilots had to keep each other within the radius at the proper range, training them to tail and target enemies effectively.*

ANSWERS:

51A. Earthquakes.

If this technology works, houses can be temporarily lifted off the ground to hover on magnetic cushions. In the case of earthquakes, the floating building will not collapse and will be safer for residents and other structures. After the tremors pass, the house can settle back on the ground again.

52A. Contact lenses.

Research indicated that tear fluids could yield good results, and new monitoring techniques are looking to develop contact lenses for regular, non-invasive monitoring of diabetic patients' glucose levels. The contact lenses would be a more convenient and less fussy way to monitor glucose levels without requiring patients to carry an additional device around.

53A. A camera.

Instead of machine guns, special cameras were mounted onto the fighter planes. These cameras were triggered just like a weapon. After the flight, the photos were checked for 'hits' to determine which pilots would be likely to shoot down enemies in real combat.

54. For a long time, there was a high demand in Europe for lamb's wool from Argentina, as a result of which lamb's meat also was popular. Besides sheep, Argentina also had large cattle production, which meant a potential for beef export. In the late 19th century, the French engineer Charles Tellier invented something that allowed shipping lines to transport Argentine beef to Europe. What invention was it?

55. During World War II, an engineer happened to walk past an active radar system with a bar of chocolate in his pocket. Strangely, the radar had a rather unfortunate effect on the chocolate - yet it inspired him to invent something that helped him make millions. Today, his invention is used in households across the world - what did he invent?

56. In Japan, a schoolboy came up with an interesting device, installed in the street outside every building. Every time a person leaves the building, a bright umbrella would open up before him. How can such a device help people?

HINTS:

54. *What is needed in order to transport meat across long distances?*

55. *A radar system consists of a transmitter that produces strong electromagnetic waves. What effect could these waves have had on chocolate, and how could it be turned to advantage?*

56. *The bright umbrella serves to grab the attention of the residents, not as an advertisement but still easily noticeable by people as they leave their houses.*

ANSWERS:

54A. Refrigerator.

Without refrigeration, meat transported long distances, especially across ocean routes, was likely to spoil. Tellier's invention allowed ships and other ocean vessels to be outfitted with refrigerating units, and this changed the Argentinian meat industry completely. Despite this invention and some awards, Tellier died impoverished in Paris, while the meat trade flourished across South America and Europe.

55A. The microwave oven.

The chocolate in the engineer's pocket melted when exposed to the radar's electromagnetic field. This effect led the engineer to believe that electromagnetic waves might have the ability to heat food, and the microwave oven or microwave was invented. First used by the military to heat and cook food, and later, adopted as a common household appliance world over.

56A. The device reminds residents to carry an umbrella along.

While exiting the building, the bright umbrella will serve as a reminder for residents to carry their umbrellas.

57. Many ingenious inventions are actually the products of unpleasant situations or accidents. Upon injuring part of his hand, dentist Fred Slack invented something that would then go on to be popular with 80% of today's American women. His invention entailed putting a piece of foil on the damaged part of the hand and adding filling material on top of it. What was this invention?

58. In carpentry, planer tools are used to smooth wood, removing rough bits and splinters without damaging the rest of the surface. In 1770, Frenchman Jean Jacques Perret designed another device, taking inspiration from the wood planer. What was this device?

59. In 2002, Canadian Wayne Fromm found himself faced with a problem as he stood in a crowd on the Old Bridge in Florence. Upon returning to his home country, he created something to solve this problem by taking apart several umbrellas and constructing something new out of them. This new invention was the first version of a modern device. What is it?

HINTS:

57. *His method created a hard and shiny material attached to the hand.*

58. *What was important was to cut only what needed to be cut and not anything else.*

59. *The Old Bridge is popular among tourists because of its gorgeous views.*

ANSWERS:

57A. False or artificial nails

Long, well-shaped nails are considered aesthetically pleasing, but real nails often wear out or break due to everyday tasks. To help deal with this problem and keep their nails looking stylish, many women turn to Fred Slack's invention: false or artificial nails.

58A. Safety razor

In 1770, French master cutler Jean Jacques Perret published "The Art of Shaving Oneself." In this book, Perret proposed (reportedly for the first time ever) the use of the 'safety razor,' or what was essentially a straight razor enclosed in a wooden frame to keep it from making deep cuts—much like carpenters' planers.

59A. The selfie stick

While traveling through the picturesque city of Florence, Fromm and his daughter wanted to capture a moment together against the backdrop of the Old Bridge. However, there was no way to mount the camera amid the crowd, nor did they want to ask strangers for help. It was because of that moment that Fromm decided to design a handheld camera mount. In 2005, he applied for a patent for the Quik Pod, today's world leader in selfie sticks.

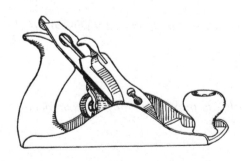

❧ IO ❧

MEDIA & ENTERTAINMENT

60. In the winter of 1977, President Jimmy Carter addressed the nation from the White House just two weeks after his inauguration. In his video message, he spoke about the country's energy security and encouraged a judicious use of natural resources. Apart from his message, he drove home his point in a rather pointed and unconventional way: by setting an example. How did Jimmy Carter appeal to the nation to conserve natural resources?

HINTS:

60. *How could Jimmy Carter set a personal example of conserving energy in his home via a video message during the cold winter months?*

ANSWERS:

60A. Carter dressed warmly for his video interview and thereby set a precedent for the nation.

While most politicians deliver official addresses in suits, Jimmy Carter donned a yellow cardigan during that winter speech. By encouraging the nation to make personal choices, like dressing warmly instead of spending resources on heating, he inspired others to make better, more environmentally-friendly choices.

QUESTIONS:

61. Every year, the final match of the Super Bowl, the American Football Championship, attracts record-breaking TV audiences, who consume huge quantities of carbonated drinks and snacks like burgers, chicken wings, among others. On the day after, economists estimate that the profits of certain companies grow by about 20% - which companies could be reaping the benefits?

62. Oscar Award-winning Maggie Smith is easily one of Britain's most famous actresses. She once offered a complimentary ticket for a play she was performing in to a housepainter working on renovating her home—an invitation that was accepted, only to result in unexpected demands later on. What did the painter ask of Smith after attending the performance?

63. Daisuke Inoue, a Japanese musician, worked as a party musician. In 1971, a client was keen that Inoue join him for a party, but he was unable to due to a prior commitment. Instead of letting down his client,

Inoue invented something that is now popular not only in Japan but all over the world. What invention is this?

HINTS:

61. *On the day of the event, the beverage and snack companies would profit the most. Yet the question asks who would profit on the day after? Who would benefit from the after-effect of such unhealthy consumption?*

62. *Not everyone is a fan of the theater.*

63. *Inoue's work was tied into the entertainment industry, and his role was traditionally very important at Japan's social gatherings. As Inoue was unable to perform, he needed to invent a device that could replace him. What device was this?*

ANSWERS:

61A. Pharmaceutical companies.

Excessive consumption of unhealthy beverages and snacks can cause serious health problems. Economists argue that pharmaceutical companies that make medicines for stomach ailments, record a 20% hike in profits the day after the Super Bowl.

62A. The painter demanded to be paid for the hours spent watching the play.

As Maggie Smith's employee, the painter mistook her gesture of generosity as a work assignment... and so, billed for his hours of work.

63A. A Karaoke machine.

Daisuke Inoue is known for his invention of the Karaoke machine - a device that reproduces melodies without voice. As a backup musician, Inoue would do the rounds with business people who wanted to sing in bars. His Karaoke machine allowed people to sing in bars without a live back-up.

64. A train carrying timber is just about to depart when you are suddenly tasked with determining the volume of wood to be transported. You have a large ruler or meterstick, so you could technically measure each log and count how many there are to calculate the total volume. However, all the logs have already been secured on the train's open flatbed cars, and the train needs to leave soon — you simply don't have time! How can you figure out a solution quickly?

HINTS:

64. *You can work on the computations after the train leaves, but what do you need to do now to make that possible later?*

ANSWERS:

64A. Take a photo of each car unit from an angle where all loaded logs are visible, with your ruler right next to the pile.

Taking snapshots — whether photo or video — with a reference scale for later analysis is a common practice among inventors and scientists. In this particular problem, the photos would show you not just the number of logs but also the diameter of each, thanks to the ruler. You can then use these to do your calculations whenever you have time, even once the train has long departed.

QUESTIONS:

65. Peter Dirichlet, the German mathematician, was considered a taciturn person. He once sent a telegram to a relative with the text '2 + 1 = 3' - what significant change in his life did he wish to communicate with this cryptic telegram?

. . .

66. Ancient Greece's Aesop's Fables are simple yet symbolic stories containing valuable life lessons. In one fable, a thirsty bird came across a jar with a little water in it. However, the water level was too low for the bird to reach. How did it solve its problem?

HINTS:

65. *What important, and otherwise rather an emotional change in one's life can be communicated through numbers?*

66. *How could the bird somehow reduce the depth of the jar to make the water level rise?*

ANSWERS:

65A. It was a laconic way of informing the relative that he had had a child.

As a mathematician, there's no better way to express addition to one's life than an equation - his wife, himself, and a child = 3.

66A. The bird dropped stones into the jar.

By filling up the volume with rocks, the bird was able to push the water upwards—to get something out, you must first put something in. This could very well be a symbolic life lesson, but did you know that this is also a common concept in inventions? For example, water is often pumped into oil wells to increase the pressure, and as a result, extract more oil. Because oil is the lighter of the two substances, it stays at the top, just like the water above stones in the ancient fable.

II

INTERMEDIATE
PROBLEMS

I WOULD LOVE TO HEAR
FROM YOU

If you enjoy this book, I'd love to hear all about it — please do leave a review on Amazon and any socials. Here is the direct link:

http://review241.inventanddiscover.com

I take great care in ensuring the books' accuracy and overall quality, and I always stay open to suggestions.

Should you spot any issues or have any thoughts on what I can do better, please don't hesitate to reach out via email or the official Facebook page.

www.inventanddiscover.com

facebook.com/inventanddiscover

amazon.com/author/inventanddiscover

goodreads.com/inventanddiscover

bookbub.com/authors/invent-and-discover

BUSINESS INNOVATIONS

67. During the early days of the British colony New South Wales in Australia, Governor Lachlan Macquarie quickly found himself faced with a major challenge: a shortage of currency. Fortunately, in the early 19th century, the government sent the colony a shipment of Spanish silver dollars which Macquarie was able to double the number of in order to overcome the coin shortage. How did he manage to do this, if all coins still had to be round?

HINTS:

67. *The coins were not thick enough to simply be sliced into two thinner layers, but they could be cut in a different way.*

ANSWERS:

67A. He ordered a hole to be punched into the center of each coin.

Punching a hole into each coin resulted in two pieces: an outer ring and a round middle piece. Both pieces were assigned a respective denomination and used as currency, effectively doubling the number of coins.

QUESTIONS:

68. Small private pig farms are faced with the problem of getting pigs to eat more and eat faster. How could an enclosure be better equipped to encourage a piglet to eat more voraciously?

69. Nobody likes waiting at an airport baggage carousel. As part of an unusual advertising gimmick, a gambling company modified the baggage carousel at a Russian airport. What changes did they incorporate which served as an advertisement, and made the wait more fun?

70. In the mid-60s of the 20th Century, Swedish authorities introduced eight thousand buses with doors on both the right and left side of the passenger compartments for a short period of time, after which they were phased out. What problem could the two-door passenger buses have helped solve?

71. A red booth installed at the trendy Café Brooklyn in Atlanta wasn't just placed for aesthetic appeal - it serves an important purpose in the busy cafe. What purpose does it serve the cafe visitors?

. . .

HINTS:

68. *Piglets tend to eat faster when there are rivals around, but how can a single pig enclosure be equipped to give the illusion of competitors?*

69. *The gambling company gamified the experience of waiting for one's luggage. What is one of the most popular casino games?*

70. *The problem was related to a transition being rolled out across the country at the time.*

71. *Historically, what did red booths signify and how can cafe visitors use them today?*

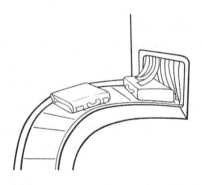

ANSWERS:

68A. By setting up a couple of mirrors.

In a small enclosure, setting up a couple of mirrors gives the pig an illusion that it is surrounded by rivals - causing it to eat faster, and eat more in a bid to secure more food for itself.

69A. The carousel was made to look like a Roulette wheel, with red and black colored numbers.

The gambling company stylized the baggage carousel into a giant casino-styled Roulette wheel, painted in numbers from 1 to 36, alternating between red and black sections. As passengers wait, they could gamble on which compartments and numbers their luggage would fall into.

70A. The two-door buses helped Sweden transition from left-hand traffic to right-hand traffic rules.

Buses with doors on both sides could not only drive on both sides of the road, they also were more convenient for passengers to board and alight from either side. Sweden introduced such two-door buses during the transitional phase between their left-hand and right-hand traffic rules for the safe, and convenient conduit of passengers.

71A. Visitors can step into the red booth to field calls on their mobile phones.

Mobile calls in public spaces can be quite disruptive. The red booths ensure privacy for all patrons of the cafe, those who need to take calls, and the others who would like to engage in conversations.

72. 19th-century shipowners in Hamburg, Germany made a lot of money off emigrants wanting to sail to America. However, Atlantic conditions in winters were severe, and passenger numbers dropped during the cold months. What idea did entrepreneur Albert Ballin come up with to ensure that ships and crews would not stand idle in winter?

73. The manager of an American bar was urged by the owner to increase the sale of their Long Island cocktails. After good, hard thinking, the manager proposed an idea to add something in the cocktail glasses that would not cost much and yet increase demand. The idea was rolled out, and sales tripled. What idea did the resourceful manager implement?

74. Years ago, the management at an American firm enrolled their group of managers for a series of courses. The courses began at 6 pm, right after the firm's working hours. While the study aimed at building specific essential skills, what was the other reason for the enrollment?

HINTS:

72. *A ship and her crew cannot be put to any other use than transportation. How can a ship continue to run in winter, perhaps sailing to locations where the weather is more favorable?*

73. *To increase the sale of cocktails, you need clients to drink faster. What could encourage clients to drink faster, and thereby order more?*

74. *The lessons were arranged off the office premises - what would a 6 pm external course mean for desk-bound managers?*

ANSWERS:

72A. He introduced sea cruises as a new type of recreation.

While most steamers and ships were used for getting from one place to another, in this case, Europe to America, Albert Ballin was the first to realize that rich people are willing to pay well for new modes of entertainment. He introduced sea cruises as a new type of recreation in the winter of 1891. In January 1891, the steamer Augusta Victora was designed as a luxury floating hotel, and the world's first Mediterranean cruise sailed for 57 days, with no empty berths.

73A. Providing a second straw with the cocktail.

The manager suggested adding another straw to the cocktails served. The extra straw meant patrons were drinking faster, and ordering more often, thereby tripling the bar's sales.

74A. Leaving work on time for a better work-life balance.

Many managers work tirelessly around the clock and tend to have a poor work-life balance. As attendance for the courses needed to be punctual, the management ensured managers learned to leave work on time, and avoid overworking and burnout.

75. In the United States, a few years ago, an argument broke out during a family game of Monopoly. One of the participants was seriously injured. To prevent such disputes in the future, the Monopoly company recruited new staff to render a free service for participants. What was the staff responsible for?

76. To encourage good behavior on the road, Stockholm traffic authorities have come up with an innovative method to reward drivers. The speeding fines are diverted for an annual event organized for drivers who have not violated any rules throughout the year. What event is this?

77. Among other marketing ideas, Steve Jobs proposed that iPods be tested in factories not just for half an hour but for two hours. While the longer test ensured the devices were of better quality, there was one other advantage. What was it?

HINTS:

75. *Most disputes in games are caused due to a misunderstanding of the rules. What simple, practical solution could the company have found to address such issues?*

76. *Good behavior is its own reward, but money could help too. How could speeding fines be used to reward mindful drivers?*

77. *The devices were hooked up to a power source during the tests. What would a longer testing time translate to?*

ANSWERS:

75A. The new staff monitored a hotline and explained the game rules to players who called in.

The manufacturers of Monopoly set up a call center and started a hotline service for players. Anyone could call the hotline, get an official answer from company representatives about the game rules, and diffuse disputes.

76A. Speed Camera Lottery.

In Stockholm, if you drove at or under the road speed limits for a year, you are entered into the Speed Camera Lottery, Sweden's innovative way to reward compliance. Rolled out to incentivize behavior change, the annual Speed Camera Lottery utilizes the fines collected from speed defaulters to reward the speed-compliant. This is among other great ideas for 'social gamification'.

77A. A full charge, and the possibility for a buyer to start using the iPod immediately.

A half an hour check would only power up the iPod partially. A two-hour test would ensure quality and charge the device completely. A buyer then had the option to start using the iPod right after purchase, which gave him a better sense of satisfaction - which underlines Steve Jobs' genius.

✿ 13 ✿
CULTURE & ARTS

78. In the mid-1990s, Walter Ostermeyer patented a new mouthpiece for clarinet reeds. While traditionally, bamboo is used to construct these musical instruments, the woody stem makes a certain essential function somewhat problematic while playing. In his opinion, the mouthpiece made playing the instrument easier and more enjoyable and facilitated an important function. His patented mouthpieces would also be more of a novelty for children. What kind of musical mouthpiece did Ostermeyer invent?

HINTS:

78. *Dry bamboo reeds are inflexible, and players are required to salivate the instrument in order to soften them and produce music. What innovation would enable this function and make playing more enjoyable?*

ANSWERS:

78A. Flavored musical mouthpieces.

Traditional bamboo reeds tend to dry out while playing, and players are forced to moisten the reed by sucking on it before and during a performance. Understandably, the bamboo reeds do not taste too good, and moistening them often becomes yet another obstacle when youngsters wish to learn the instrument. Ostermeyer's flavored musical instrument reeds contain a reservoir saturated with flavoring and food coloring, which ensure salivation. The reservoir is designed to last as long as the bamboo reed itself, and makes it easier for both children and adults to play the instruments.

QUESTIONS:

79. In the spring of 1842, star composer and pianist of the time, Franz Liszt, came on tour to Russia. As is usually the case even with modern musical celebrities, the public not only wanted to be able to listen to him play but also see his performance. Even those with front row tickets wanted to get as close as possible to him while he played. This posed quite a challenge, as his concert was held onstage in a huge, wide hall. How did they remedy this?

80. In 1969, Austrian-born American photographer Inge Morath and her husband, playwright Arthur Miller, published 'In Russia.' These compiled visual works and diary entries documented Morath and Miller's travels through the Soviet Union. In the book, Morath recalls how she often had to listen to classical music while visiting Russian friends. Why was that necessary?

. . .

81. Timeline of the Future, a book written by the Japanese journalist Masashi Kawai, delved into a serious social problem for Japan at the time. Masashi illustrated the problem with a sheet of paper, with instructions as follows: take the sheet, fold it in half. Then fold that half into another half...and so on. What social problem was Masashi Kawai trying to illustrate in this fashion?

82. French artist and designer Antoine Tesquier Ted (also known simply as Tes-Ted) has created a series of stickers depicting specific everyday objects, such as a phone, driver's license, keys, some money, and a pair of eyeglasses. Where are these stickers recommended to be affixed?

HINTS:

79. *Only audiences near the piano would typically have a clear, unobstructed view of the performer—how did they give more members of the audience this same proximity in a very wide hall?*

80. *This music was played very loudly, which helped Morath and her Russian friends talk amongst themselves.*

81. *Each time a sheet is folded into half, it becomes twice as smaller - what social problem could be illustrated by such reductionism? Several countries in Europe and others like Korea and Cuba have realized this problem in recent decades.*

82. *The objects depicted are all things people often forget.*

ANSWERS:

79A. Two grand pianos were put onstage for Liszt's concert.

To give the entire audience—no matter where in the hall they were seated—the opportunity to enjoy watching his performance, Liszt played half of his concert on a piano on one side of the stage and the second half on the other.

80A. To keep their conversations private, safe from eavesdropping neighbors and even spy bugs or wiretapping

At the time, USSR was a totalitarian country. Morath and her friends played loud classical music to drown out their conversations. So, should the walls have ears, they could still feel safe discussing anything and everything freely, including sensitive political topics.

81A. Japan's population decline problem.

In his book, Masashi Kawai tried to demonstrate how quickly Japan's population decreases if most couples only have one child. With each generation, the population of Japan will halve! As per his calculations, by the year 3000, Japan's population will only be 2000 people.

82A. At the front door

Like many of Tes-Ted's other works, these stickers merge decorative aesthetics and functionality. The series, called "Before Leaving," is meant to be displayed stuck by the front door to remind people not to forget the essentials when leaving home.

14

CUSTOMS & TRADITIONS

83. In ancient China, ancient death rites once dictated that all possessions be burned along with deceased persons to provide them with the comforts they enjoyed while alive. However, as the burning was rather expensive, the rites were later amended, though their essence remained unchanged. How were the death rites conducted thereon, where the burning continued but incurred lesser financial burden upon the deceased's family?

HINTS:

83. *The revision in death rites employed another Chinese invention known to change the world. What is ancient China known for, and how could the invention transform death rites into something more symbolic?*

ANSWERS:

83A. Instead of burning possessions, a list of all the possessions was drafted onto strips of paper, and the paper was burned instead.

The invention of paper is credited to ancient China, first made with mixed mulberry bark, hemp, and cloth rags pulped and dried out into thin mats. To avoid burning possessions, the Chinese dictated that death rites involve writing out lists on strips of paper. Then as a symbolic offering, the paper was burned instead.

QUESTIONS:

84. In Mandarin, the language spoken by the Chinese, the Kanzi characters often represent more than one word. The character for 'cheerfulness', can also be used for one other word, about which Chinese say 'it strengthens the spirit, softens the heart, removes fatigue, lightens and refreshes the body. What word could it be?

85. When the world was just being created, and the stars took their places in the sky, a chow-chow dog was allowed to lick a piece of the sky, which fell to the ground, reads a Chinese legend. What peculiarity of the chow-chow dog does the legend go on to describe?

86. In the Polynesian islands in the Pacific Ocean, certain tribes follow a strange tradition. To prove that he is not yet too old or too weak to lead, the chief of the tribe must present a symbol of his vigor to fellow tribesmen every now and then. What symbol of plant origin does he present?

. . .

87. In classical Japan's Heian period, noble samurai Taira no Masakado led the first-ever recorded uprising against the government in the country. Upon his victory, he declared himself emperor—a political move challenged by many. Once, a courtier meeting with him for negotiations came to the conclusion that Masakado couldn't possibly be the emperor. This realization dawned on him upon noticing Masakado drop several grains of rice on his clothes and proceed to brush them off with his hand. According to tradition, what should a real emperor have done in such a situation?

HINTS:

84. *The word talks about a food product that is well-known throughout the world.*

85. *The answer lies in the color of the sky.*

86. *The symbol is something that grows profusely on the Polynesian islands, and procuring it would be a show of strength.*

87. *A true emperor must not concern himself with such mundane things.*

ANSWERS:

84A. Tea or chai in Chinese.

China is well-known for its tea, and beyond being a part of their routine, it is also consumed for physical and mental well-being. Where else in the world would the words for tea and cheerfulness use the same characters?

85A. The chow-chow dogs have a distinct bluish-purple tongue.

The chow-chow dog breed originates in northern China, and along with a sturdy build, broad skull, and triangular ears, it has a distinct bluish-purple tongue. The legend tries to explain why the dog's tongue is that peculiar color.

86A. A coconut.

If a leader could periodically present a coconut that he had picked himself by climbing the high reaches of a coconut tree, he could prove that he was still fit and able enough to lead his tribe.

87A. Order a servant to remove the spilled rice

Especially when it came to royalty, ancient Japan was governed by hierarchy and propriety. According to the traditions of the time, a real emperor was not to deal with such small matters since there were servants at his disposal.

88. In some traditions, if a child in a particular family falls sick, in certain cases the family invites other children for a party. The party features games and goodies, and all the children play together with the sick child. Why would parents send their healthy children to such a party?

89. In the 1940s, the USA gained administration over Micronesia. As part of this, Americans built schools across the islands, bringing Western education to the locals. A new custom then arose among some local men: when courting ladies and inviting them on dates, these men would write their beloved not just one but several letters at once. Why would they do this?

90. According to Sumerian legend, a wild boar mortally wounded by hunters threw himself into the sea. Since then, the Sumerians and all other people follow a particular custom related to their food. What is it?

HINTS:

88. *What sickness is better experienced in childhood, than in adults? How can the party help?*

89. *With the arrival of Westerners, the rules of conduct and social interaction on the island also changed.*

90. *This is a rather elaborate legend for a common practice since the early days of hunting. How can seawater translate into a common routine related to food?*

ANSWERS:

88A. To contract chickenpox.

If a child in the neighborhood is down with chickenpox, other children are invited to play and party. A quickly spreading chickenpox infection in the children ensures lifetime inoculation and immunity, thereby encouraging such parties. An early infection confers resistance against this disease through adulthood, but adults without such immunity often face complications.

89A. To save time in case girls initially refused

Men were taught that it in 'civilized' society, it was considered too eager and somewhat indecent for ladies to respond to the first and second notes. Sending several letters at once would allow women to maintain propriety without men wasting time on their initial refusals!

90A. People started adding salt to their food.

Legend claims, that when the hunters pulled the boar carcass out of the water, the salty water had added some taste to the meat. Since then, people salt their meat before eating - and today, we cannot imagine eating meat unsalted.

91. Legend has it, that a system in China, traces its origins to the practice of fortune-telling using a turtle shell. The shell was heated over a flame and sharply cooled in springwater. The bizarre cracks that appeared on the shell were interpreted by priests as a divine oracle. What system originated in such a manner, and is still in use today?

92. Jainism, a religion founded in India, is based on the tenets of virtue, honesty, and respect for every form of life, as well as 'ahimsa', or non-violence. To better uphold these tenets, devout Jains wear light, white masks that cover their noses and mouths. How do these masks help them adhere to their principles?

93. In the olden days, peasant families in Belarus baked a large number of bread loaves - one of which was marked with a cross. What did the loaf with a cross signify?

HINTS:

91. *What could cracks resemble? How did this practice lead to meaningfully interpreting the patterns of cracks?*

92. *In Jainism, even the life of insects is respected.*

93. *The loaves were baked for several days or weeks at a time. The cross mark helped the family to plan ahead.*

ANSWERS:

91A. The characters of the Chinese writing system.

The cracks in a rapidly cooled shell would represent the logograms that later formed the Chinese language script. Sometimes mistakenly referred to as 'hieroglyphs', there are over 20,000 Chinese logograms.

92A. The masks prevent Jains from breathing in and killing small insects, by filtering them out.

The concept of 'ahimsa', or non-violence also stretches to include all forms of life. Taking the life of any creature, no matter how accidental, is considered to be a crime. The mask not just serves to filter out tiny insects, but also as a reminder for when they speak - to ensure, they do not speak anything hurtful or harsh.

93A. The last bread loaf in the larder.

When the bread loaf with a cross on it was placed on the table, it would be the last one left in the larder. The peasant family would either have nothing more to eat or would need to bake a new batch on the following day.

15

FOLK WISDOM

94. In the olden days, a covering of pitch or tar was commonly used to protect wooden ships from rotting in water. During his first trip around the world, famous European explorer Ferdinand Magellan once found himself in need of this protective substance to maintain his ships. So, upon arriving in the Philippines, he asked the locals to bring him some, explaining what he needed it for. What did they bring him instead?

HINTS:

94. *Natives to the island also had boats, so they understood the importance of protection and in fact had methods of their own. Instead of pitch, they gave Magellan a product of their own technology—a substance they had in abundance in the country.*

ANSWERS:

94A. Coconut oil

Today, coconut oil is better known as a natural sunscreen and skin-care ingredient. Back then, though, because of its excellent water repellent properties, it was also used by many pacific islanders to protect wooden boats and ships against rot. However, treating huge European ships with it would have been too expensive due to the lack of local supply in their countries compared to tropical islands. In fact, to this day, the Philippines remains a key exporter of coconuts and coconut oil to the rest of the world, including Europe.

QUESTIONS:

95. In the Middle Ages, infusions of herbs like hemlock, opium, henbane, and hemp were often used by doctors as anesthesia. The patients were administered the infusion orally, or a sponge was soaked into the infusion and burned during surgery and the patient would be lulled to sleep with somniferous vapors. However, the latter method posed a hilarious yet serious problem and had to be abandoned. What problem could burning the sponge have caused?

96. In the month of Ramadan, Muslims are forbidden from eating during the day. However, they may start cooking their feasts to break the fast with. While how well rice has cooked can be judged by squishing a grain of rice between two fingers, there is another important factor involved in making pilaf or spiced rice. Experienced chefs can still cook the perfect pilaf by watching the bubbles as it boils. What are they able to deduce from watching the rice cook?

. . .

97. Togunu are special houses built with canopies of dried millet sheaves raised from 8 pillars. The Dogon tribe in Africa gathers under the 'togunu' to tackle important issues. As important issues are likely to cause disagreements, the togunu have a unique architectural feature to discourage or prevent fights. What feature is this?

98. In some desert regions of North Africa, households maintain an even spread of fine sand just outside the doorways. Why do you think residents do that?

HINTS:

95. *To ensure the patient is constantly under anesthetic, the soaked sponge had to be burning throughout the surgery. What possible result could this have had?*

96. *The chefs cannot eat during the day and thereby, cannot taste the food they prepare. The size and number of bubbles vary as per the chemical composition of rice and water, a difference that can usually be detected by tasting. How can merely watching the bubbles allow chefs to cook the perfect pilaf?*

97. *Think of the posture most men assume while fighting - what feature in construction can restrict men from assuming that posture, and thereby discouraging a fight?*

98. *The residents keep a wary eye on the condition of the sand and take care not to step on it, hence the sand doesn't serve to clean their feet or footwear.*

ANSWERS:

95A. Often, the doctor fell asleep with the patient while inhaling the fumes.

Administering the herbal infusion to the patient orally would mean that the anesthetic acts only on the patient. Burning the soaked sponge, however, had the undesirable effect of inducing sleep in both the doctor and patient, and therefore had to be abandoned.

96A. The amount of salt in the pilaf.

Experienced chefs who may usually judge a dish by its taste, look instead at the size and number of bubbles while boiling rice - the more the salt, the lesser the bubbles. This careful observation allows them to deduce the amount of salt in a dish without tasting it, and yet turn out perfect pilafs.

97A. Togunu have low ceilings which cause a man to stoop, instead of standing upright.

Posture is important for fighting, you need the full height of your body, and the space to move your arms and legs to their fullest extent - architecture that prevents disputants from standing upright, is likely to prevent a full-blown fight.

98A. To track if a snake has entered the house

When slithering in, the snake is likely to leave a trail in the sand, and residents can be wary of it. Interestingly, border checkpoints employ a similar technique to identify illegal migrations.

99. The Nogais are a Turkic ethnic group that inhabits the north Caucasus Mountains, and some of them can trace their ancestry to Genghis Khan. As pastoral folk, their tradition involves a curious practice: if a mare dies during childbirth, her surviving, newborn foal is tied to a post, and dogs are let loose near it and even encouraged to bark. The experience would be quite terrifying for the newborn. Why would the Nogais follow such a strange custom?

100. Shibam, a city in Yemen bears the epithet, "Manhattan of the Desert". The houses in this city are multi-storied buildings, and have high-ceilinged rooms with an unusual arrangement of windows: for every large window located near the ground, there's another smaller one located high up, almost under the ceiling. What purpose do these two windows serve?

HINTS:

99. *As an orphan, the newborn foal would find it difficult to survive without a mother's instinctual, instructive care. Strange as it sounds, this custom actually improves the foal's chances of survival.*

100. *Interestingly, this arrangement of windows is also seen in houses from ancient times. Architects of yore had found a way to harness the laws of physics, to ensure the comfort of residents. How could these windows make the residents of a desert city more comfortable?*

ANSWERS:

99A. If threatened, the newborn foal may stir maternal instincts in other nearby mares, who would fend for it, and thereby start taking care of it.

If an orphan foal is not adopted soon after the death of its mother, its chances of survival are bleak. The dogs circling and barking at the newborn, can awaken the maternal instincts of a nearby mare, and this attachment and need to protect proves vital for the foal.

100A. By facilitating natural air ventilation.

As per the laws of physics, hot air rises, while cold air sinks. In the hot Yemeni desert, the lower windows let in cool air, which forces the hot air to rise and escape through the upper windows, thereby providing a natural, cooling mechanism for the buildings.

101. Without modern tools, craftsmen in ancient civilizations were resourceful, innovative thinkers who worked with whatever was readily available to them to create extraordinary results. For example, Syrian blacksmiths, who were famous for their skill, used the sun. To create some of the best, most sought-after swords in the ancient world, Damascus steel swords, they looked at the sun at sunset during a particular stage in their forging process. Why did they do this?

102. There is great danger involved in shoeing a horse's hind legs - the horse is likely to kick the farrier. How does the blacksmith's assistant ensure the horse cannot kick the farrier with its hooves?

103. Historically, the Nama people of the southern African countries were pastoralists, or cattle herders, a role they still practice. Oddly, on their farms, one is likely to see baboons. Why are the baboons around?

HINTS:

101. *What happens to the sun's appearance at sunset?*

102. *With four hoofed legs and the ability to kick with all legs, the only way to curb a horse's desire to kick would be for the blacksmith's assistant to make the horse realize that it cannot do so safely? What simple trick is used to do this?*

103. *The baboons on the farm were not wild, they were tame and trained - what could the baboons have been trained for? Remember, the Nama people are pastoralists, which means their farms are likely to have livestock.*

ANSWERS:

101A. To ensure proper hardening, they heated steel until it took on the color of the sun at sunset.

Steel must first be heated to a thousand degrees Celsius during hardening to increase its strength. At this temperature, it takes on a specific color—this color was observed by ancient Syrian blacksmiths to be the same as that of the sun at sunset. So, before the advent of thermometers, these metallurgists perfected their steel hardening process by using the sun as a gauge.

102A. The blacksmith's assistant lifts and holds up the shin of the front leg that is diametrically opposed to the one being shod.

As the farrier lifts one leg to fix it, his assistant lifts the opposite one - in effect, the horse stands on just two legs and is unable to kick as it would lose balance.

103A. As shepherds.

While most countries use dogs as farm shepherds, the farms of the Nama people in southern Africa use baboons. Baboons are rather smart creatures and can be trained to help herd goats and cattle, prevent fights among the herds, and warn of predators approaching.

104. The Great Wall of China was built by Chinese emperors to protect their territory. Along the inner perimeter of the wall, holes were dug into which huge drums were placed. Dry peas were then scattered over the top of the drums. Why were these drums an essential part of China's defense system?

105. The Arctic and subarctic regions are some of the coldest zones in the world, with temperatures dropping as low as −45 °C (−49 °F). Indigenous people in these areas, the Inuits, often prefer to build their igloos on the frozen surface of the sea rather than on land. Why is this?

106. In some dry regions of Iran, pomegranates flourish. The locals have mastered the art of eating pomegranates without getting the sticky juice on their fingers and can save water by not needing to wash up after. How do the locals eat pomegranates without touching the juicy grains?

HINTS:

104. *A certain kind of lookout and monitoring was essential to protect the wall, but logistically, it just wasn't possible to station soldiers around its entire perimeter*

105. *Land and water are fundamentally different in terms of certain physical properties, making houses built on the latter much more comfortable.*

106. *How can you eat fruit like a pomegranate without peeling it and getting your hands messy?*

ANSWERS:

104A. The drums amplified any underground activity, such as vibrations from enemy digging, and served as an alert system for defenders within the wall's perimeters.

If enemies tried to dig their way into China, ground vibrations caused by their activity would be picked up by the large drums, causing the peas on it to rattle. This noise would then alert Chinese soldiers of the potential attack.

105A. The sea is warmer.

Water retains heat for more extended periods than the solid ground because it has a higher heating capacity and allows heat to penetrate its depths through convection. So, Inuits noticed that temperatures on water are higher than on land despite the frozen surface.

106A. The locals crush the pomegranate without cutting the peel. Once the grains inside turn to liquid, a small hole is made and the dark juice can be drunk from it.

Anyone who has peeled pomegranates would know just how sticky the juice is, and how difficult it is to get at the ruby berries. Crushing the fruit while it is contained by the peel, and then making a hole in it, is a less messy way to eat the pomegranate.

16

HISTORICAL HAPPENINGS

107. Every Christmas, the Pope broadcasts live to Christians all over the world from the Vatican. In 1974, the broadcasting team faced a serious problem: they required additional wiring for their set-up. With time of the essence, an engineering platoon from the Italian army was dispatched to help out the Vatican. However, the commander of the papal guard, Franz von Altishofen, was forced to refuse the troops of another country to enter his territory, as it would constitute a military incursion. As the commander Franz was eager to allow the army platoon in without dishonoring the military protocol, he merely set them some conditions - what did he propose?

HINTS:

107. *What militarily acceptable solution could be offered from the commander of one territory to an army platoon of another that could not be construed as an invasion or attack?*

ANSWERS:

107A. Commander Franz proposed that the Italian platoon surrender.

To uphold his military rank as commander of the papal guard, Franz could not allow the Italian army platoon to 'invade' the Vatican. The Vatican is an independent city-state, surrounded by Rome, in Italy. To ensure that the deployment of the Italian army is not construed as a military offense, Franz proposed that the platoon surrender, help install the electrical wiring, and would then be sent back by the 'victors' - the Vatican papal guards.

QUESTIONS:

108. The Romans trace a lot of their martial traditions to their deities. There is a legend behind the 'aegis' - the shield carried by Zeus, gifted to Rome by the gods themselves. Every March, a collegium of twelve priests sworn to guard this relic hold a parade through Rome - with one of them holding the sacred shield aloft. The priests are not armed with weapons. Despite the danger of carrying such a precious object into a public space, they believe it is impossible to steal the shield - what do the other eleven priests carry to ensure the safety of the legendary shield?

109. In times of war, unique skill sets that enable combatants to deal with unexpected tough circumstances are often an advantage. In World War 2, one such skill elite Japanese pilots were trained with was quickly locating stars and constellations and using them to find their bearings even while turning in all directions. Aside from navigational expertise, this also helped them develop exceptional eyesight. What exactly was it about this particular training that made it extremely diffi-cult, and later on, immensely beneficial during military operations?

. . .

110. Life in the former Soviet Union was quite tough, with the government strictly implementing various rules that curtailed citizens' civil rights and certain freedoms. One such restriction involved maintaining neatly plowed strips of land along borders—first along the Soviet-Polish border, then later on, around the entire Soviet Union. What were these plowed strips of land for?

HINTS:

108. *The safety of the legendary shield lies not so much in protection, as deception.*

109. *The main objective was to develop 'superhuman' eyesight for use in battle later on. What would make it even more difficult to find stars in the sky?*

110. *It was ordered that these strips of land be plowed often so that any disturbance in the earth could be spotted immediately.*

ANSWERS:

108A. Facsimiles of the shield.

    The annual parade of the 'aegis' has twelve priests carrying twelve shields through the streets of Rome - one among which is the relic, the others are near-identical copies. Hence, making the theft of the real shield more difficult, and improbable.

109A. They were trained to be able to do it in the daytime

    Did you know that many of the brightest stars are actually visible in the daytime? However, finding these does require intense training—like that of the Japanese WW2 pilots. Developing phenomenal eyesight then helped them spot the enemy long before the enemy saw them and to notice even the subtlest details during battle, giving them the upper hand.

110A. To detect illegal border crossings

    During the Iron Curtain regime, these were known as control-and-trail strips. Human footprints show up very easily in freshly plowed earth, so officials would use these to track down spies entering the borders and defectors trying to escape.

111. The 1912 eruption of the Novarupta volcano in Alaska was powerful, and the nearby Kodiak island was covered with a 30 cms layer of ash. More than 50 years later, the smoke emissions from the crater subsided, and the location served as a backdrop for unusual training. What training was this volcanic site used for?

112. In the 18th Century, Earl William Douglas of Scotland won an unusual bet concerning velocity. A ball with paper packed inside was tossed along a human chain formed by several dozen cricketers and managed to surpass the speed of another, more commonly used means of transmission. Whose speed did this human chain manage to beat?

HINTS:

111. *The terrain of a volcanic site often seems otherworldly with its barren landscapes, and lack of vegetation. What group training could it be a backdrop for?*

112. *The ball contained a letter - what other channels were used to convey messages quickly?*

ANSWERS:

111A. Lunar landing.

In the 1960s, when the American government was preparing for an expedition to the moon, the Novarupta site in Alaska, proved ideal to train astronauts and test technology for a lunar landing.

112A. Carrier pigeon.

The earl had wagered that he could make a letter travel fifty miles in less than an hour without the help of carrier pigeons. By tossing the ball with the letter inside via a long-distance human chain, the crick-eters managed to surpass the speed of carrier pigeons - the preferred, and fastest means of delivering messages at the time and thereby helped the earl win the bet.

113. Up until the 1950s, South Africa had a large illiterate population, most of which lived in rural areas. At one point, social workers compiled a list of major or catastrophic events that occurred during the 19th and 20th centuries such as the death of a well-loved king, a plague of locusts, the appearance of Halley's comet. How could such a list have helped the officials?

114. The attack on Pearl Harbor was one of the most disastrous events in World War 2 American history. After the attack, authorities feared for the security of the country's major ports. To safeguard New York Harbor, the US Navy turned to port workers' unions for help, but this turned out to be insufficient. A certain group then stepped up, coming to the military's aid to organize securing the port in the shortest possible time. Who were they?

HINTS:

113. *The events listed were memorable events and their dates and would likely have been remembered by the population despite being illiterate. How could such events have helped social workers document the population?*

114. *These people had been (and would remain to be) in control of large ports for a couple of decades. Although this influence was under the table and largely considered unwelcome by the government, it was undeniably beneficial in this particular circumstance.*

ANSWERS:

113A. To conduct a population census.

Most people associated their children's birthdays with an important historical or political event rather than the year itself. By having a dated list of such significant events, the social workers could calculate backward to determine the dates of birth of the illiterate populace and their ages. The list helped add valuable demographic criteria to South Africa's population census.

114A. The Mafia

During Prohibition in the 1920s, the New York mafia came to be in control of most of America's major harbors. It was through seizing these ports that they oversaw the underground delivery of alcohol from Europe. As illegal as it was, this nationwide network of organized crime was precisely what put them in the position to quickly mobilize an armed guard at the Port of New York.

115. World War II not only involved military conquests but also saw the rise of technologies used for psychological intimidation. Among these intimidation tactics, Germany's bombing of Great Britain was especially effective. What small object did the Germans attach to their bombs to ensure maximum psychological impact?

116. In February 1942, the British newspaper Daily Telegraph announced a competition, for which about three dozen applicants showed up to the editorial office to participate. They were then given 12 minutes to complete a particular task. A few weeks later, contestants who succeeded at this task were invited by a representative of the British General Staff to work on a matter related to national security. What were they initially asked to do during those 12 minutes in the Daily Telegraph editorial office?

HINTS:

115. *A similar idea was used in some of Alfred Hitchcock's films. Loud, high-pitched sounds in his horror movies effectively created panic.*

116. *What does a newspaper contain that could reveal skills useful in relation to national security?*

ANSWERS:

115A. A whistle.

When attacking civilian areas, the German bombs with a whistle attached to them created a terrifying, high-pitched sound, and destruction followed. It was not long before the people started associating the sound of the shrill whistles with danger, and would panic at the sound of bombs whizzing down.

116A. Solve crossword puzzles

Solving crosswords (and quickly, no less) takes a certain methodical line of thinking, which the Daily Telegraph tested participants on in the guise of competition. They were later offered jobs on a team assigned to decoding encrypted German data transmitted by radio.

17

HOW'D THEY DO IT?

117. Chocolate candies filled with fruit syrup have long been a favorite among children and adults alike. Yet when confectioners first thought of creating such a candy, they faced a conundrum: how can thick molasses be contained within a chocolate shell? If you make a chocolate shell, the fruit syrup is too thick and does not flow - making it hard for the syrup to be poured into the chocolate casing. Heating the syrup makes it flow better, but hot molasses would cause the chocolate casing to melt. Eventually, they stumbled upon a solution - how do you think they did it?

HINTS:

117. *Turn the problem over on its head: if you can't pour the syrup into the chocolate, can you pour the chocolate over the syrup, and yet create the desired shape and size?*

ANSWERS:

117A. Confectioners froze the syrup into the desired form and then poured chocolate over it.

Molten chocolate will eventually harden around frozen syrup, and stay firm even at room temperature. The frozen syrup inside, however, will melt at room temperature, resulting in the delicious fruit syrup chocolates that we enjoy.

QUESTIONS:

118. Camera surveillance captures only visual cues, yet can it be used more effectively to apprehend crimes? In 2013, authorities in Oaxaca city, Mexico ran an interesting experiment: they hired twenty employees with a special set of skills to monitor camera footage from hundreds of devices set up across the city. The team was able to apprehend dozens of carjackers, drug dealers, and other lawbreakers. What special skills did the employees have that made them so efficient?

119. World War I saw the first use of chemical weapons, and tear gas was among the chemicals used. The armies in every country were looking for ways to counter such attacks. For example, Russian soldiers laid out armfuls of brushwood along the edges of trenches that faced the enemy ranks. How did this help counter the enemy attacks?

120. During the 2020 coronavirus pandemic, it was difficult to convince people to stay home. Students at an advertising school in Miami stumbled upon a creative, mischievous solution - informative billboards that were periodically updated, sourced mostly from Netflix

to deter people from leaving the house. What information could these posters have borne to have such an effect?

121. Certain objects intended for family homes are subjected to rigorous test trials. Each object is set on fire, torn, squeezed by a press, and even gutted, its shape is carefully examined for sharp edges, and its chemical composition is assessed. What category of household objects undergo such due process?

HINTS:

118. *Camera surveillance allows you to watch people and their behavior, but not hear them. How can you apprehend criminals with silent video footage?*

119. *Brushwood doesn't absorb the gases, but how else can it help prevent the gases from reaching those inside the trenches?*

120. *What keeps us hooked to Netflix shows that could potentially be disrupted by informative posters?*

121. *The trials are undertaken to ensure that the objects are safe, and cannot injure the users.*

ANSWERS:

118A. Lip reading.

The employees hired were lip readers, most of whom were from the deaf and dumb community. By monitoring the camera footage from across the city, and 'reading' the conversations, the team was able to apprehend several criminals. What's more, this experiment also provided meaningful employment to deaf and dumb people.

119A. The brushwood was set on fire when a gas attack was underway.

When the gas attack started, Russian soldiers set fire to the brushwood laid out at the edge of the trenches and crouched at the bottom. The brushwood blaze would burn the incoming gas, and as hot air rises upwards, both the fire and the poisonous gases would be carried upwards, and the soldiers down in the trenches would be safe.

120A. The posters featured spoilers for Netflix films and TV series.

The intrigue of storylines and characters keeps us hooked to TV shows. Most people hate spoilers, as they give away key details of the shows, and kill the suspense. The students reasoned that posters with spoilers would discourage people from going out onto the streets.

121A. Kids toys.

As per international standards, most kids' toys undergo rigorous testing for fire, hazards, chewing, and tough playing. The shape needs to have no sharp edges that could cause cuts, and the chemicals should be safe enough to chew upon. The objective of such tests is to ensure the children playing with the toys are not injured or poisoned.

122. A storm at sea may last for several hours, yet life on the ship must continue uninterrupted. When the seas are roiling, sailors use wet towels to ensure one of their routine activities is not disrupted. How do the wet towels help?

123. Several years ago, Ghana introduced a law for spouses seeking a divorce, which would help the couple remember one of the happiest days in their lives and perhaps reconsider their decision. What does the law dictate about the appearance of the estranged couple at the proceedings?

124. To make flying safe and enjoyable for everyone, flight attendants are trained to follow various protocols across different aspects of the trip. When it comes to serving food to the first and second pilots of the aircraft, what rule do flight attendants of all American airlines strictly observe?

HINTS:

122. *Wet towels may help prevent something from being tossed or moved about when the ship is in turmoil.*

123. *The assumption is that the wedding day was one of the happiest days in the couple's life. How could the law help the couple reimagine that day?*

124. *If there's something wrong with the food, flight attendants fear that pilots could get poisoned.*

ANSWERS:

122A. The wet towels help keep plates of food steady.

When the ship pitches around during inclement weather, sailors lay wet towels out in a crumpled, untidy fashion on the table and then place plates of food on top. The crumples ensure that there is friction between the plates and the towel. This way, the dishes do not slide off during upheavals, and sailors can eat their food without disruptions.

123A. The law states that couples attend their divorce proceedings dressed in wedding outfits, to recreate the day they tied the knot.

By demanding couples wear their wedding outfits, they are more likely to remember their happy moments and will hopefully reconsider their decision to get a divorce.

124A. The pilots are served two completely different sets of food.

The chances of something being wrong with all the food products are next to none. So, by feeding the pilots different sets of food, the flight is still guaranteed at least one capable pilot even in the event of poisoning.

125. In Cuba, in the 1960s, there were increasing attempts by local residents to flee to the United States across the Guantanamo base on the island. The Cuban authorities decided to create a natural barrier to prevent such escapes, much like the Berlin Wall in Germany. What did they use to build this barrier, to make it even more efficient?

126. At the World Athletics Championships in Japan, organizers provided the marathon spectators with an object. The spectators were encouraged to use it while the athletes ran the track. What object of oriental origin could have helped the marathon runners?

HINTS:

125. *The material is natural, grows widely across Cuba, and is perfect to deter escapees, as it is difficult to climb over.*

126. *The object helped give a sense of movement to the marathon runners.*

ANSWERS:

125A. Cacti.

The Cuban authorities planted a wall of cacti - there couldn't be a more effective, or prickly barrier to prevent escape through the Guantanamo base.

126A. A handheld fan.

The Japanese are known to be hospitable people. During the marathon, spectators close to the racing track were encouraged to lightly fan the athletes to make it easier and cooler for them to run.

18

HUMAN BEHAVIOR

127. Before electronic means of communication were established, the US Post offices had long queues outside. As the customers spent a long time waiting for services to be rendered, they turned indignant and registered complaints to the office. The US Post mitigated the complaints in a clever, ingenious, and a rather ironic way. What change at the post office, that did not involve hiring more staff or spending more money, allowed them to address this issue?

HINTS:

127. *The customers were indignant at the amount of time they spent in queues. What change could make the problem of waiting less obvious, reduce the indignation, and thereby complaints?*

ANSWERS:

127A. The removal of wall clocks.

As people queued up at the post office, they were wont to look at the wall clocks and realize how much time they had wasted. This caused a flurry of complaints. To make customers less anxious, the US Post offices did away with their wall clocks - the less the customers knew, the less they worried. This strategy is not likely to work in this day and age of smartphones, but then nor do we use the post office as much either.

QUESTIONS:

128. In the early 90s, Toledo Express Airport in Ohio enjoyed a significant increase in inbound and outbound flights. However, with this, the city government began receiving complaints from residents of the neighboring area. In response, the mayor proposed a solution that not just angered the local community, but also caused outrage among members of the nationwide organization No Barriers. The group snidely remarked that next, the mayor might invite blind people to work the night shift. What was the mayor's proposal?

129. The founder of a casino in Monte Carlo, François Blanc established a system to counter one of the common problems faced at casinos. There is an emergency button installed under every casino table. If the dealer sees fit, he may press the button, and immediately a specially-trained team from the casino's security staff is deployed to deal with a particular client. What service does this team render at the casino?

.   .   .

130. In the mid-1950s, a firm in Naples occupied the first and sixth floors of an old building, with a rather slow elevator. The employees complained to the management and demanded a high-speed elevator. As the complaints involved the long waiting period and installing new, a more modern elevator would have been too expensive, the management came up with a simpler and cheaper solution. It seemed to do the trick, and the complaints reduced. What did the company install?

HINTS:

128. *People living near the airport found the constant noise from continuous flights to be disturbing, especially at night.*

129. *The problem is related to how clients deal with a loss at the casino table. How can the security team help?*

130. *Most employees in the firm were women, and the installation was perfect to distract them from noticing how long they had to wait.*

ANSWERS:

128A. To settle deaf people in homes near the airport

In response to residents' noise complaints, the mayor proposed to move deaf people—who obviously would not be disturbed by the airplanes' sounds—into the homes nearest to the airport instead. "No Barriers," a society advocating for people with disabilities, called him out for this insensitive move.

129A. The team may prevent suicide from occurring when a client loses.

Often when people lose a lot of money, they despair. Some choose to end it all and may attempt suicide as a permanent step to their temporary problem. If the dealer notices distress signals in clients, he presses the button, and the specially-trained security team steps in to counter any suicidal attempts.

130A. A mirror.

Instead of installing a new elevator, the management turned to psychologists who advised them to install a mirror. When stuck in a hallway waiting for a slow elevator, the employees could switch their attention to the mirror instead, and save the company the cost of a new elevator.

131. Becoming great at anything takes practice and preparation. In the past, it was common for students preparing for a certain profession to keep a thread in their pockets. Without taking it out, they would use this thread to practice tying knots with one hand. What future occupation were these students aspiring for?

132. In England, in the country of Yorkshire, there is a sleepy, little town called Waite. While most pubs shut early, one stays open till after midnight - and the post-midnight patrons are given a lollipop while exiting. Why do the pub staff dispense lollipops at this late hour?

133. Experts suggest that parents present their young children with any of these specific items: a bottle and its lid, a pair of scissors and a piece of paper, some thread and a needle, or a bell. According to researchers, doing so would help parents identify something in their kids early. What is it?

HINTS:

131. *They did this to train their finger flexibility and ability to make knots in hard-to-reach places.*

132. *No matter the age of the patrons, anyone handed a lollipop is likely to immediately consume it. How can this help the pub stay out of trouble?*

133. *Parents only need to observe their children as they perform the simple actions these items require.*

ANSWERS:

131A. Surgeons

Medical operations often entail tying off stitches, sometimes with limited visibility and access. Not to mention, finger dexterity and flexibility are generally essential for any surgeon. Practicing manipulating thread in their pockets helped medical students—future surgeons—train their fingers and practice their skills.

132A. Drunk patrons with a lollipop in their mouths are less likely to sing or talk loudly, and disrupt the peace in the sleepy town.

Drunk patrons of pubs are best known for their loud, raucous behavior. To ensure minimal disturbance to the residents of Waite, the pub dispenses lollipops to hush patrons.

133A. Right- or left-handedness

These items require simple, intuitive actions to manipulate. Parents can determine their dominant hand early on by simply observing which hand their kids naturally use when presented with these objects.

134. Recently, Chinese authorities in Chongqing ran the experiment of divided pedestrian paths in the busiest parts of the city. While it is easy to switch from one track to another, what distinction can there be between pedestrians to cause them to change tracks?

135. Every year, over 35,000 climbers flock to Mount Everest to scale the summit - at a price! In addition to the fees to climb the mountain, Nepal authorities recently enforced a security deposit of $4000 per group of climbers to tackle a serious problem. What is expected of the climbers to ensure the return of their security deposit?

HINTS:

134. *As with all traffic, the difference between pedestrians would be that of walking speed - how would two tracks help? What modern-day lifestyle pattern would cause a change in the pace of pedestrians.*

135. *The climbers are expected to bring back something from their expedition that ensures the ecological balance at Mount Everest.*

ANSWERS:

134A. The two tracks were created to separate pedestrians walking while using their mobile phones from others, walking without distraction.

Mobile conversations and text messages tend to slow pedestrians down. Chongqing's authorities divided the pedestrian track to allow those using their mobile phones to slow down while leaving a track for the faster, undistracted pedestrians.

135A. To return with all their trash.

Years of expeditions have caused a severe garbage problem at Mount Everest, and the sherpas who lead the alpinists are forced to clean up after. The environmental security deposit dictates that each climber bring back 8 kilograms of garbage, either from what they have carried or that of other climbers, to ensure the return of their security deposit. The authorities hope that this will mitigate the garbage problem at Mount Everest and ensure the trails are left more pristine for climbers in the years to come.

19

I WONDER WHY...?

136. A residential neighborhood in Amsterdam is lined with uniform houses, all built at the same time, each with one family in it. Despite these similarities, a 1970s study showed that the electricity consumption in these houses differs significantly: with some homes consuming over 3 times the amount of others. Oddly, the consumption pattern had little to do with the number of residents. Instead, they found that it had to do with the location of the electricity meters. What was different about the houses that consumed lesser electricity?

HINTS:

136. *While the houses and the electricity meters were similar (though the location of the meters might have differed), the consumption patterns were linked to the psychology of people.*

ANSWERS:

136A. Houses with electricity meters located in plain sight consumed lesser electricity than houses where meters were placed in less accessible places, like the basement.

If houses had electricity meters that were visible and might have served as visual reminders, families were better able to assess the costs, and consume economically. In homes where the meters were difficult to access, families consumed less carefully and thereby had higher bills.

QUESTIONS:

137. In the 19th century, transactions at pet bird markets were conducted in this manner: sellers would ask buyers "would you like to take the bird out from the cage yourself, or should I?" Why would seasoned buyers be wary of sellers touching the bird they wanted to purchase, and prefer to take it out of the cage themselves?

138. Through the ages, money has been the motivation behind bizarre bets. In the 19th century, a prankster took on a challenge at a restaurant: he claimed that he would ensure the guests would not drink water all evening. The prankster entered the restaurant, ordered some water, and invited guests to use a 17th-century invention he had carried along. Strangely, no one wanted to drink the water after that. What invention helped the prankster win his bet?

139. When the first tenement houses were built in ancient Rome, they often had four or eight stories. The apartments, each of which had its own wooden staircase, were rented out to both rich and poor people.

The separate staircases offered an ingenious solution to a common problem faced by the landlords. What problem could they have addressed?

140. During the 19th century, soldiers in North Caucasus were known to be brave, strong warriors in their fight against invading Russians. Notably, many of these Caucasian military men wore a massive ring on the thumb of their right hand. Though these could be ornate in appearance, these stemmed from a purely utilitarian purpose. What was this purpose?

HINTS:

137. *This precaution ensured that buyers would trust the seller, and would return to him in the future. Whereas buyers would prefer handling the birds themselves to avoid dishonest sellers.*

138. *The invention did not involve any addition to the water, yet it made the guests squeamish about drinking it. What 17th-century invention could have such an effect?*

139. *The staircases weren't just separate, they were also foldable and movable. The problem is still faced by landlords today and has to do with guarding their financial interests.*

140. *These soldiers were armed with small weapons.*

ANSWERS:

137A. Caged birds that were handled often died early, as unscrupulous sellers would imperceptibly pinch the bird under the wings and cause internal bleeding. Buyers were urged to handle the bird themselves. To maximize profits, unethical sellers would pinch the pet bird under the wings before handing them over to the buyer, knowing that they would be forced to return to the market shortly after. By asking buyers to handle the bird themselves, sellers could establish their reputation, and could also avoid being blamed later for a bird that might die suddenly.

138A. A microscope.

The prankster had mounted a slide with water samples from the restaurant on the microscope - guests peered in to see the water teeming with micro-organisms. This made the guests too squeamish about drinking the restaurant water. In the 19th century, most people did not know that water, even potable water was full of microscopic life, and hence the prankster managed to win his bet.

139A. When a tenant evaded payment, the landlord could remove the staircase leading to the apartment and prevent the tenant from escaping.

As the apartments were rented to both the rich and poor, the landlords ran the risk of poorer tenants evading payment. Movable, foldable staircases ensured that the landlord always had the upper hand, and could coerce a tenant into paying up rather than escaping.

140A. To cock the hammer of their weapon's trigger

North Caucasian soldiers carried flintlock rifles, which at that time had small, tight hammers that were notoriously difficult to cock without a ring.

141. In Denmark, forest rangers spray trees with a special temperature-triggered substance. In the cold, the substance is virtually undetectable. Once indoors at room temperature though, it starts to give off a foul stench. What purpose does this serve?

142. In China, in the olden days, incense sticks were widely used. Each stick bore regular, precisely calculated notches. These incense sticks were used in temples, mines, and even while brewing tea - what possible use could these notched incense sticks have served?

143. Our modern lifestyles have ushered in a new range of health issues. Some small children display strange symptoms: when facing an obstacle, they tend to jump in place rather than over it. Or when navigating certain spaces, the child turns only the head instead of the entire body. What do doctors prescribe eliminating from the life of youngsters to fix these problems?

HINTS:

141. *Forest rangers only spray the trees during a short period of time in the winter. How does this seasonal treatment help protect forests?*

142. *The keyword here is olden days. Incense sticks burn slowly, much the same way as candles do. Today, we use more sophisticated technology for the same purpose.*

143. *Consider the symptoms carefully; where would such unnatural movements be used?*

ANSWERS:

141A. To prevent illegal logging for Christmas.

Denmark is one of the world's largest producers of natural Christmas trees. Unfortunately, with this vast market come poachers. To prevent illegal felling of these firs, forest rangers use a unique substance that doesn't affect trees outdoors in the wild but turns foul indoors at room temperature. Not only would house guests automatically be able to spot an illegally obtained tree, but also, who would want a stinky holiday celebration?

142A. To measure time intervals.

Incense clocks were used widely during the Song dynasty in ancient China to measure time. Sticks could either be cut to the desired length to tell the elapsed time, or notches would be cut into the sticks to mark time intervals. Incense sticks could also be used as alarms, where bells were attached to the incense stick. When the stick burned down to the attached level, the bell would fall off and ring.

143A. Computer or video games.

Young children who play virtual games for long hours tend to display strange symptoms that mimic the movement of their gaming characters. Controlling the moves of virtual characters requires minimal physical movements, and children tend to be disconnected from the real world. Doctors suggest a complete break from the computer or video games to address these issues.

144. During the Napoleonic wars, French soldiers seized numerous estates that were abandoned hastily by fugitive owners. After seizing the estates, the troops poured water all around the grounds, in search of something. What could they possibly have been searching for, and how would pouring water have helped?

145. Around the world, currency comes in many different shapes and sizes. In the 20th century, coins in Iraq, Pakistan, India, and Sierra Leone were a bit different from the typical round coin. Each denomination came in a distinctive geometric shape, such as a pentagon or a hexagon. Thinking about what these countries had in common, what was one reason behind the unique coin shapes?

146. The Pentagon complex has not only offices of the US Department of Defence. It also houses many banks, shops, and restaurants. There are flower, confectionary, and jewelry shops in the Pentagon lobby, which, as the inside joke goes, sometimes are no less essential than the defense offices. Why are these shops considered necessary?

HINTS:

144. *The soldiers were observing how the water was absorbed into the ground. Can the speed of absorption provide any clues?*

145. *All these countries had a high level of illiteracy in the 20th century.*

146. *The Pentagon has a huge male workforce, most of whom work late into the night.*

ANSWERS:

144A. Buried treasure.

The former estate owners would have been forced to travel light with a hasty evacuation. The easiest way to hide treasures before fleeing would be to bury them, which was what Napoleonic soldiers were keen on. As freshly dug soil absorbs water more quickly than hard, compacted soil, pouring water all around the grounds would have helped the soldiers to locate buried treasure.

145A. The distinct shapes of the coins allowed people to distinguish their value or denomination without having to know how to read the numbers.

While the high illiteracy rate in these countries was the primary reason behind this, if you thought of blind people, you're also right— unique geometric shapes help the visually impaired tell the denominations apart through touch alone.

146A. After late working hours, men often need to bribe their way back to their wives, with flowers, candy or jewelry, as the occasion demands.

There are many work hazards for Pentagon officials, among which, the joke goes, are unhappy, waiting wives. Therefore, the flower, confectionary, and jewelry shops are necessary for those working late at the Pentagon to make amends at home.

147. The USA maintains over 2 million miles of pipelines for natural gas transmission, spread out across the continent. Pipeline workers in the United States add a chemical that smells like rotting meat to the natural gas. This smell attracts vultures from far and wide. What purpose does this tactic serve?

148. The Russian Empire's currency was traditionally made of gold, silver, and copper, but in 1828, they minted the world's first platinum coins. These coins of 3, 6, and 12 rubles were in circulation for years and became greatly prized by the upper class. Merchants and other wealthy citizens often used these particular coins to store their savings. Why did they especially value these platinum coins?

149. Some hotel rooms in the world, have not just one number plate on the door but two, both with the same number, of course. One number plate is located at eye level, whereas the other is located halfway to the floor. Why would a hotel door need two number plates?

HINTS:

147. *What is a common problem faced by pipelines? The engineers use this tactic to help them deal with this problem.*

148. *What physical property does platinum possess that sets it apart from gold and silver?*

149. *The second number plate is not intended for children (though it could serve that purpose), but is visible if guests are crouching in the corridor on all fours.*

ANSWERS:

147A. To locate the leak in a pipeline.

Vultures flock to the smell of rotting meat. The chemical added smells like rotting meat and attracts the vultures from far and wide, who circle the source of the leak. A flock of vultures with their large wingspans makes it easier to locate the source of the leak in the pipeline unless there's also a rotting carcass nearby!

148A. Platinum's melting point is much higher than that of other precious metals.

Upperclass citizens of the Russian Empire preferred to store their savings in the form of platinum coins to ensure that in case of fire, their wealth would be kept intact.

149A. For better visibility in case of fire.

Most fire evacuation protocols in hotel corridors advise people to crawl on all fours as they make their way to the exit. This is especially helpful if there is heavy smoke. The lower number plates allow the evacuees to determine which way the fire exits are, and move towards them.

150. In 1776, the English Admiralty issued orders for the ropes used in the navy to be woven with a red thread. The factories that made such rope, followed the instructions, and the red thread was woven in such a way, that it could not be removed. What was the need for such custom-made ropes?

151. The writer and educator, Ibuka Masaru noted that during the first six months of training as antique dealers, students are surrounded by valuable, genuine works of art. What's more, beyond merely appreciating them, they were encouraged to make copies of these pieces. Why are they encouraged to do so?

152. When buying tickets for a corrida or bullfight in Spain, you have a choice between the grandstands - the western stand costs more than the eastern stand. Why would these tickets be priced differently?

HINTS:

150. *The key lies in not being able to unravel the red thread from the strong navy rope. This addition served no direct practical purpose; it was just bright and visible. How could this feature of the ropes have helped?*

151. *What knowledge would the students acquire by making copies of genuine works of art?*

152. *Most bullfights happen in the evenings. The key lies in Spain's location in south Europe.*

ANSWERS:

150A. To fight against theft - stolen rope interwoven with red could not be sold.

To counter theft of navy ropes, the English Admiralty ensured their ropes were made with a unique, and easily identifiable feature: the red thread.

151A. In order for students to distinguish genuine antiques from fakes.

The master Japanese antique dealers hoped that an environment of both authentic pieces and replicas would allow students to develop a keener eye to distinguish between fake and genuine antiques and inculcate a greater sense of appreciation for true masterpieces.

152A. The western grandstand is in the shade, whereas the eastern one is sunny.

Spain is a sunny country located in southern Europe. In the evenings, with the sun dipping towards the western side of the sky, the eastern grandstands are bright and sunny. At the same time, the western grandstands are in the shade. As the sun shining in one's eyes is not the best view for any sport, the shaded western grandstands cost more.

153. One of the world's most famous left-handers was the Rennaisance polymath Leonardo da Vinci. In addition to using his dominant hand to write, da Vinci also devised a unique style of jotting things down—he wrote in mirror image, from right to left. While keeping his manuscripts encrypted was one reason for this, what was another purpose behind it?

154. In ancient times, prison perimeters were patrolled not just by guards but also by horses. Once a month, a horse was led around the prison walls, and this practice still continues in some parts of the world to date. What purpose could such a horse patrol serve?

155. So the story goes, a speeding driver was pulled over by a Belgian police officer and asked to produce a driver's license. Instead, the driver held out a banknote. Oddly, he was neither charged for not producing a valid license, nor for offering a bribe. Why?

HINTS:

153. *In those days, writing was done in ink.*

154. *Horses are sensitive animals and can feel danger - they are not likely to walk over ground that seems unsafe.*

155. *This incident happened in the last century, and the policeman duly checked the banknote and handed it back. Why would he have done so?*

ANSWERS:

153A. To avoid smearing or smudging his writing

Especially for left-handers, ink was known for being notoriously easy to smear while writing. With his right-to-left method, da Vinci was able to avoid having to move his hand over what he had just written on the page, helping prevent smudges in the drying ink.

154A. To determine if prisoners have built tunnels underground for jailbreaks.

An underground tunnel makes for dangerous terrain. If a horse senses a hollow space underground, it is not likely to walk over it. Thereby, as a prison patrol, the horse can pre-empt jailbreaks via tunnels.

155A. The driver was the king of Belgium.

The banknote presented to the police officer bore a photo of the king Albert II, and thereby, the king was able to prove his identity without a license, nor needed a bribe to be let off free.

156. Finland's traffic statistics indicate a higher incidence of winter road accidents, than at other times in the year. One of the causes identified was reindeer on the roads. Why would reindeer venture onto the roads more often in winter?

157. American car brand Dodge is known for its high-performance sports cars and trucks. For a certain valuable demonstration though, the company has also designed a car with intentionally delayed steering and braking systems. What is it meant to show?

158. In 1977, in the Taranaki province of New Zealand, cows began to exhibit strange symptoms. The farmers feared it was a new virus, but veterinarians linked the symptoms to welding work happening on a gas pipeline nearby. To address the problem, one Auckland company proposed an unusual solution - what solution did they offer?

HINTS:

156. *Could there be something different about the roads during winter that attracts reindeer?*

157. *The goal of the demonstration is to help resolve a prevalent social problem by making people realize something important.*

158. *The cows suffered from poor eyesight as a result of watching the welding work. What solution could work for such symptoms?*

ANSWERS:

156A. In search of salt.

In winter, the roads are sprayed with salt. Salt prevents ice forma-tion by reducing the freezing point, thereby preventing dangerous ice from accumulating on the streets. In the cold forests, salt is in short supply, and reindeer venture out onto the roads searching for salt.

157A. The slow reaction time of a drunk driver

According to many studies, alcohol severely impacts reaction time. With a special car designed to simulate this effect, Dodge aims to educate and campaign against drunk driving and its potentially disas-trous consequences.

158A. Sunglasses for cows.

This unusual problem required a creative solution. Sunglasses would have dimmed the welding torches' glow and protected the cows' eyesight.

159. In Germany, many motorways have automated signs with photosensors. If the sensor detects fog, the sign shows a speed limit of 40 km/h. The system works rather flawlessly, yet on one clear, sunny day, a sign indicated the unnecessary speed limit. What could have caused such failure?

160. In England, in the mid 18th century, the hulls of ships were sheathed with copper sheets to protect them from water and marine organisms. In 1764, the 'Dolphin' - the first-ever vessel with a sheathed hull, returned from a voyage much faster than usual and still in excellent condition. However, the sailors on board the 'Dolphin' had faced one major problem: sheathing made performing one essential, routine activity difficult. Why were the sailors displeased?

161. The Nigerian wrestler Amalinze earned the nickname 'Cat' for a skill that rendered him invincible in the ring. What skill was this?

HINTS:

159. *The system relies on the photosensor to detect weather conditions; which creature was responsible for fogging up the system in clear weather?*

160. *Copper sheathings would have been brighter than the traditional wooden hulls, as they reflected the sun's rays. This had the unfortunate effect of causing the sailors to go hungry sometimes. Why?*

161. *When is a wrestler considered defeated? What cat-like skill could help him avoid defeat?*

ANSWERS:

159A. A spiderweb.

The photosensor could not detect the ambient conditions as its screen had been covered with cobwebs, thereby giving a false reading.

160A. The shiny, new copper sheaths scared off the fish and made it difficult for sailors to enjoy their pastime and catch fare to vary up their meals.

Despite being underwater, copper sheaths would have glinted in the sun and caused fish to panic and dart away. The sailors were unable to fish onboard and add variety to their meals. Therefore they returned from the voyage a little disappointed.

161A. Amalinze never fell on his back - he always managed to land on either his hands or feet.

When a wrestler lands on his back, the opponent has the chance to pin him down and claim victory. Amalinze was nearly invincible in the ring and earned the nickname 'Cat' with his unique ability to always land on his hands or feet.

INGENIOUS INVENTIONS

162. In the 1970s, the Soviet Union was planning to send the Lunokhod rover to the moon. The Lunokhod was equipped with an incandescent lamp, which had a weakness at the point where the bulb was attached to the base. However, during the hard landing tests of the lunar rover, the delicate glass bulb was unable to withstand the impact and kept falling off. Remember, the LEDs we use today were not invented yet. Finally, an innovative solution was found to ensure the lunar rover could be illuminated after a rough voyage. What solution did they arrive at?

HINTS:

162. *Why is a glass case or bulb required for an incandescent lamp? What function does it serve?*

ANSWERS:

162A. The glass bulb was abandoned, and just the light-emitting filament was mounted onto the rover.

In an incandescent lamp, the glass bulb contains an inert gas to prevent the filament from burning out. A lunar rover was not likely to encounter atmosphere on the moon. In the absence of oxygen, which causes filaments to burn, the glass bulb was no longer necessary to protect the filament. The lunar rover was fitted with just a filament instead. New contexts often need new ideas rather than repurposing or rehashing old ones. This is a perfect example where a new context allowed a simpler, and more elegant solution to emerge.

QUESTIONS:

163. Much of the technology we enjoy today actually has roots that stretch as far back as centuries ago. In Ancient Greece, a slow-moving contraption was invented to make it easier to transport goods. Over time, this underwent several iterations, improving with the advancement of technology. Still, it wasn't deemed safe enough for transporting humans—malfunctions could be dangerous, even fatal. Its use often remained limited to carrying goods until the mid-19th century, when a revolutionary safety system was invented for this machine. This system finally made it safe for people to use as well. What is this contraption?

164. American-British inventor Hiram Maxim invented the gun silencer. Gun silencers reduce the acoustic intensity of gunshot sounds. They work by slowing down the turbulence of gases after a bullet has been fired. Hiram's invention stems from an everyday observation at home that sparked the idea of how to slow down gases and dampen the sound of a muzzle blast. What observation inspired him?

. . .

165. With the advent of aviation, aircraft wings were still undergoing transformations. They were attached to the hull with steel bracing straps, and their tension had to be finely balanced: a weak tension caused the wings to vibrate dangerously, a stronger tension could cause the braces to break mid-flight. To help solve this issue, Russian professor Vetchinkin invented the 'monochord' - a device that could check the tension of the cables. However, the device could only be used by people with a particular natural ability. What ability was needed to master the 'monochord?'

HINTS:

163. *In case of breakage, overloading, or any other accident, this machine could lose control of its acceleration. It was the development of a brake system to counter this that made it safe for human use.*

164. *Hiram found his inspiration in the bathroom! What observation in the bathroom allowed him to watch how airflow can be slowed down by forcing it to pass through a longer route?*

165. *As with any adjustment of tension-based devices, the key lies in vibrations. A tight brace would vibrate at a frequency higher than a loose brace.*

ANSWERS:

163A. An elevator

Elevators function via a pulley mechanism. If the cable were to snap or malfunction, the cabin itself could plummet dangerously. As a safeguard against this, inventor Elisha Otis developed a reliable emergency brake that would automatically stop the elevator immediately in case of cable failure. To this day, safety systems based on Otis' are what make it safe for elevators to be used for moving both goods and people.

164A. The bathtub drain - which can be unplugged and the water to be flushed out slowly, silently, in swirls.

There's more than 1 eureka moment that happened in a bathroom. When the bathtub plug is removed, water swirls, thus going a longer route. As a result, it makes its way out slowly and silently. Could small guns be equipped with an airflow swirler to dampen sounds? That's what Maxim's solution to the muzzle blast was - a gun silencer is often a metallic cylinder lined with mufflers, with a single borehole running through. This borehole allows the bullet to fire through with little resistance, yet the gas that it ejects is forced through a longer, denser escape route - this helps muffle the sound as well as reduce the recoil.

165A. A good ear for music.

Vetchinkin's 'monochord' device consisted of strings stretched across a resonating board, tuned to the frequencies of normal, optimal-tension braces. To compare the frequencies and pitch of the device with that of the braces on the aircraft wings, one needs to perceive minor sound differences to deduce the tension of the wings. A good ear for music was essential for mastering the 'monochord' and fine-tuning the balance of the aircraft wings.

166. The construction of a dam on the Connecticut River was widely viewed as an environmental problem - it was difficult for local fish to navigate past the high walls to lay their eggs upstream in familiar, shallow pools. As the local fish could have been threatened with extinction, an innovative solution that costs several million dollars was found and implemented close to the dam. What innovation was this?

167. Ever been stuck on a problem and stumbled upon a solution in a dream? That's exactly what happened to Elias Howe - his invention was missing something, and the answer came to him in a dream: he was surrounded by savages armed with spears, each with a hole at the sharp end of it. They were stabbing the spears into the ground repeatedly - up and down. Upon waking, Elias realized just what his invention needed - what did he invent?

HINTS:

166. *What innovation that is often used by people, would also allow fish to move upstream with a mechanical assist?*

167. *Think of what the spears with holes and their repeated stabbing motion could signify? In which invention have you seen something similar, albeit at a different scale?*

ANSWERS:

166A. Fish elevators or lifts.

To help fish surmount high dam walls during their spawning period, dams across the United States have installed mechanical elevator-like contraptions - fish are channeled into hoppers and raised to the level of the dam wall, where they can continue to move upstream. Endangered species like American shad and Atlantic salmon, among others, have been assisted in their efforts to breed in the shallow pools that they are drawn to during their spawning season. However, in more recent years, the efficiency of these elevators has been called into question, and other solutions are being sought.

167A. Sewing Machine.

The spears with holes at the end inspired him to design the needles with eyelets, and the repeated stabbing motions helped him understand how a threaded needle could make lock-stitches in a moving fabric. Much to his dismay, Elias Howe's lock-stitch sewing machine, which was the more successful than previous designs, was later copied by Isaac Merritt Singer. The Singer sewing machines are still among the most popular brands nowadays.

168. In 1832, before metal cartridges existed, an Egyptian gun crew discovered that they had a better firing rate if gunpowder was encased in paper sleeves. This innovation was well-received, and they were awarded a special ration of a product that was quite popular among soldiers at the time. To make the ration easier to consume, the soldiers employed the same technique they had used for the gunpowder. This might have been among the first samples of what is today a 5.5 trillion unit industry. What product did the soldiers pioneer?

169. In 1989, while watching TV reports of a huge oil spill in Alaska, Phil McCrory found himself particularly drawn to coverage of oil-soaked sea otters. Inspired by this, he got to work on a new method for removing oil products from water. After some experimentation, he soon introduced his proposal to the public. According to Phil's calculations, his colleagues would be able to produce about 100 tons per day of the main component needed for this new water purification method. What industry was McCrory in?

HINTS:

168. *Alcohol* was *often doled out to soldiers to keep them warm, and happy. What other 'ration' serves a similar purpose - and how is it consumed today?*

169. *It all started with McCrory's observation of how difficult it was to remove oil from the sea otters' fur.*

ANSWERS:

168A. The soldiers were awarded tobacco, and they might have created the first-ever cigarettes.

Some say that these soldiers made the first cigarettes by twisting tobacco into paper to make it burn better and easier to carry around than a traditional smoking pipe. This innovation of pre-packing tobacco into paper sleeves helped spawn an industry that kills over 7 million people worldwide each year.

169A. McCrory was a barber

Upon seeing how oil-absorbent the otters' fur was, salon owner Philip McCrory began to wonder if human hair was the same. After years of further research and development, he patented two devices that used human hair for cleaning up oil spills.

170. In Cologne, Germany, the traffic lights at busy intersections seem to work quite normally at most times. However, there are instances when by design the red light stays on for longer, and the flow of cars is diverted to neighboring streets. What could cause such a strange occurrence?

171. In 1816, the French physician Laennec was watching children in a nearby courtyard play with a hollow log. One child would scratch at one end of the log, the others would listen intently at the other end. This inspired him to invent a device based on the same principle - what device was it?

172. Until the mid-1900s, an object bore three of these features. After the Italians began to add gloopy tomato sauce to the pasta, four features became standard - what commonly used object, and its features could this be?

HINTS:

170. *The traffic lights are 'smart', they are tuned to certain changes in the traffic and the environment, and their erratic behavior helps address a crucial urban problem.*

171. *The hollow log would have amplified sounds from one end as they reached another. What medical device allows physicians to use this kind of amplification for diagnosis?*

172. *This is related to how we eat slippery pasta, especially spaghetti.*

ANSWERS:

170A. A change in air quality triggers the traffic lights to change their behavior.

The 'smart' traffic lights can detect air pollution levels in busy streets. Suppose the air quality dips below a healthy level. In that case, the traffic lights stay red for longer, diverting the vehicles to adjacent streets, thereby temporarily reducing vehicle emissions in the monitored place. After the levels are in check again, the traffic lights return to regular work, till there's another spike in air pollution.

171A. A stethoscope.

Often a medical checkup includes auscultation - the action of listening to the sounds of internal organs such as the lungs and heart. Changes in the usual rhythm of these internal organs were previously diagnosed by the physician placing their head on the patient's chest. The invention of the stethoscope by Laennec was an important milestone in medical sciences, as it made auscultation more precise and convenient.

172A. The tines on a fork.

Italians, and now people from all over the world, eat spaghetti by wrapping it around a fork. It was difficult to roll up the spaghetti with three-pronged forks with a more gloopy sauce, and the four-pronged ones were introduced.

173. Sometimes, the simplest things can inspire life-saving solutions. An engineer once witnessed a fatal accident, and as a result, devoted his efforts to finding a solution to avoid similar situations in the future. The right idea finally came to him when he saw a woman on the street pull a large silk shawl from her tiny handbag. What did this engineer invent?

174. In 1904, Thomas Sullivan, an American merchant changed the packaging of a popular product - from the traditional tin or wooden cans to silk bags. This innovation created quite a stir and changed the way the product was consumed. What product did he revolutionize?

175. The inspiration for inventions can be found in the strangest of ways. It is said that a Hungarian journalist was watching children play with a ball after the rains. As the ball left wet, dirty marks on the ground, the journalist was inspired to invent something. What invention was it?

HINTS:

173. *The key was being able to pack a large piece of material into a small space.*

174. *Interestingly, the silk bags allowed the product to be consumed as is, without unpacking.*

175. *The key lies in how a wet ball leaves traces on the ground while rolling. The invention helped the journalist in his work and is widely used today - you have undoubtedly used it too.*

ANSWERS:

173A. The backpack parachute

Having witnessed a fatal plane crash in which the pilot could not escape the falling aircraft, engineer Gleb Kotelnikov resolved to develop a life-saving device for similar accidents. Ultimately, it was seeing a woman pull a large scarf out of her handbag quickly that made him find the solution. Gleb realized the advantage of using durable yet light silk (instead of heavy tarpaulin) for parachutes that could then be compact enough to be worn in knapsacks.

174A. Tea.

Sullivan's new silk packaging allowed customers to brew the tea directly in the bag. Teabags have since become a more popular and more convenient way to consume tea.

175A. A ballpoint pen.

In 1938, the Hungarian journalist Laszlo Bíró invented the ball-point pen - inspired by the wet trail left behind by a rolling ball. The traditional fountain pens had liquid ink that leaked onto the paper through a thin groove and they were a messy and inconvenient way to write. The ballpoint pen has left a legacy across many industries since.

176. The University of Tokyo has developed a special fork for hypertension patients - those suffering from high blood pressure. Upon pressing a button while eating, the fork sends weak electrical impulses to the tongue that stimulate the taste buds. The signals trick the patient into feeling there is enough of a particular ingredient in the food - what is the fork trying to compensate for?

177. Novuss is a game that's very similar to billiards or pool games. Unlike billiards though, it is played on a smaller table, one meter by one meter, and with small discs, or pucks, instead of balls. What profession gave rise to this game about a hundred years ago?

178. The 1950s were a prime time for technological innovation. In 1955, the Zenith Radio Corporation invented a device that was indeed useful but had unexpected consequences. Scientific studies later showed that because of this device, obesity rates doubled over the span of 10 years. What is this invention?

HINTS:

176. *Electric impulses to the tongue can modify the sensation of taste. What taste do the electric impulses mimic, that patients suffering from high blood pressure are advised to avoid?*

177. *Unlike balls, the flat pucks do not roll, even when the table is tilted.*

178. *This small device can be found in almost every home.*

ANSWERS:

176A. The taste of table salt.

Hypertension patients are advised to stay away from salty foods and to follow a low-sodium diet. As salt is an essential ingredient in most food, and the lack of it would make food seem tasteless and unappetizing, the fork stimulates the tastebuds in a way that they cannot detect the deficiency.

177A. Sailors

A century ago, billiards gained immense popularity. However, sailors found that not only was the table too big for their meeting rooms, but also, the balls rolled all over the place with the movement of the ship. To be able to play their favorite game, they devised a smaller table and replaced the balls with discs, inventing what is known today as novuss.

178A. The TV remote control

TV remote controls are incredibly convenient, but this convenience is precisely what contributed to the rise in obesity. Not only did people just start flipping through channels without having to get up and go to their TV sets, but as a result, they also began to spend more time watching.

179. A famous businessman started out as a traveling salesman. As a frequent train traveler, he noticed that passengers on long-haul journeys often found it difficult to perform one particular morning routine, often at the risk of serious injury. He was inspired to invent something that would be more convenient for travelers. What was it?

180. Inspiration for inventions sometimes comes in the most unexpected forms. Take Swiss engineer George de Mestral, for instance. Upon arriving home from walking his dog through the countryside, de Mestral found himself having to pull out burdock burrs that had gotten stuck in the animal's fur. This spurred the invention of something we use to this day. What was it?

HINTS:

179. *The risk of performing routine procedures on trains is due to the train's strong translatory or side-to-side motion. What invention could minimize such danger?*

180. *Burdock is a weed that's common in fields and grassy areas or paths. Its little brown burrs have tiny hooks that allow these to stick infuriatingly to fuzzy surfaces like socks, pant legs, and your dog's fur. Annoying as these may be, de Mestral saw the potential to use these for something beneficial.*

ANSWERS:

179A. A safety shaving razor.

Every day, male train passengers needing a shave used old-fashioned razors and were in constant danger of accidental nicks and cuts to their throats. The traveling salesman named Gilette invented the safety razor that was a safer, more convenient way for men to groom on board a train; and went on to found a business worth billions.

180A. Velcro

The mechanism behind Velcro is essentially the same: one side has rows of tiny hooks just like a burdock burr, and the other side is furry or fuzzy, allowing the hooks to latch on.

181. In the Middle Ages, certain measurements were made by watching the movement of materials like fried and grated eggshells, or zinc and lead dust. The Danish astronomer, Tycho Brahe, suggested mercury as an alternative. Where were these materials being used, and what did they measure?

182. It is well-known that rodents are prone to the annoying habit of chewing on any electrical wiring they have access to: in homes, cars, or anywhere else they might nest. In the 1990s, inventor Frank Etscorn proposed an interesting solution to this problem—one that was completely environment-friendly and would not harm the animals. What was his solution?

183. Between 1950 and 1980, Florida moved up the list of most populated states, from rank 20 to 4. Some scientists correlate this dramatic influx of population to Florida to the popularization of an earlier technology, which in the 1950s became more compact, afford-able, and free of toxic substances. Which invention was this?

HINTS:

181. *The materials listed are free-flowing, quite like sand or water. What can be measured through such movement?*

182. *What can be added to the wires' plastic insulation to discourage animals from biting it?*

183. *What technology might influence more people to choose Florida's weather?*

ANSWERS:

181A. In an hourglass to measure the passage of time.

In the Middle Ages, hourglasses were filled with eggshells or zinc and lead dust. These were tested to pass from the upper chamber to the lower to determine which substance had the more consistent flow. The rate of flow allowed the hourglasses to measure time. Mercury, or quicksilver, with its heavy flow, was suggested as an alternate, and later, special kinds of sand were used for the same purpose.

182A. Pepper extract

The hot, spicy taste of pepper is thanks to its capsaicin content. Treating wires with a high enough concentration of this extracted substance, or even cheaper synthetic versions of it, makes it unpleasant for rodents—or any animals, for that matter—to chew.

183A. Air conditioners.

With the widespread adoption of air conditioners, more residents from the northern states of America were willing to move to the southern, sultrier parts of the country. This may have been one of the major reasons for the boom in Florida's population. Having no state tax is definitely a perk too!

MEDIA & ENTERTAINMENT

184. Today, one can find mobile applications that help you learn almost anything. One such app teaches magic tricks that you can show to a circle of friends and is widely used by illusionists. However, a study found that despite wide usage, good quality, and usefulness, the app is rated quite poorly in the app stores. Why does the app receive a poor rating from budding performers?

HINTS:

184. *The answer lies in the reluctance of illusionists to share their secrets.*

ANSWERS:

184A. Poor rating for an app means it features further down the app store lists. Illusionists rate the app poorly so that their friends and competitors do not stumble upon the same tricks.

Mystery is an essential part of the illusionist's stock-in-trade. Mobile apps have opened up a new avenue for learning magic tricks and are readily available to everyone. By providing low ratings for good quality apps, trick performers hope that it will not appear in the recommendations; so they can hold onto their secrets.

QUESTIONS:

185. In 2008, Nik Wallenda, an American acrobat was the first to cross the Grand Canyon on a tightrope, earning him the nickname 'The King of the Wire'. To prepare for his daredevil feat, Wallenda had to factor in a natural phenomenon and used a special installation to help him simulate the right conditions. What natural phenomenon did he have to account for?

186. A creative advertisement poster of a car company bore the slogan: "No surprises after purchase". Interestingly, the poster also featured a mid-fall vegetable - which vegetable could reinforce the company's slogan about buying a car you could depend on?

187. There is a TV network in Toronto, Canada, that only features media that are no more than 5 minutes long. Basically, its programming consists of just news clips and commercials. This channel is only broadcast in certain spots — the spaces that many of us likely use daily. Where is the channel shown?

. . .

HINTS:

185. *For a tightrope walker across large stretches of open terrain such as the Grand Canyon, what natural phenomenon would interfere with your ability? Nik used a special device, similar to the one most people have at home but much stronger, to account for this.*

186. *Think back to your childhood, is there a story that made you think that a vehicle could suddenly disappear or transform?*

187. *The station's programs are only a couple of minutes long because audiences are only around for extremely short periods of time.*

ANSWERS:

185A. Wind.

The high wire artist, Nik Wallenda trained for his Grand Canyon feat by using a large fan that simulated the crosswinds that he would face.

186A. A pumpkin.

The poster harks back to the story of Cinderella, where the fairy godmother turns a pumpkin into a golden chariot. At the stroke of midnight, the chariot turns back into a pumpkin! The car company wanted to reinforce that their cars would come with no surprises after purchase.

187A. In elevators

Many elevators have screens on which videos can be played. These are extremely hot real estate for advertisers, as people are essentially captive audiences for the duration of the ride.

NATURE & SCIENCE

188. Along the banks of Siberian rivers, loggers would stack logs to be transported to timber mills downriver. To the surprise of the loggers, a bear wandered by, picked up some logs, and started to throw them into the water. It returned almost every day and continued doing the same. It was only when some of the loggers saw the bear again further downstream that the reason for its strange behavior became apparent. Why was the bear throwing the logs into the water?

HINTS:

188. *The behavior of animals is often dictated by their needs, in this case, hunger. How could the bear throwing logs from a height have helped the bear find food?*

ANSWERS:

188A. To stun the fish in the water for a while, and hunt them.

Tool usage in animals is always a surprising and remarkable behavior. The bear was using the logs of wood in much the same way illegal fishermen use dynamite - a large log falling into the water creates a strong sound wave which stuns fish for a while, making them an easier catch for the bear to collect further downstream. When explosives are used for fishing, the technique is known as blast fishing.

QUESTIONS:

189. Animals are often equipped with natural defense mechanisms against predators and enemies. One well-known example of this is how many cephalopods such as squids and octopuses emit inky liquid to envelop themselves in a dark veil that effectively hides them from enemies' view. However, in waters deeper than a kilometer, sunlight is virtually absent. In this pitch-black environment, predators hunt by spotting their prey's bioluminescence (light-producing properties). Leveraging this fact, how then do deep-water cephalopods use their liquid-emitting ability to protect themselves?

190. Some sandgrouse birds live in the dry, arid habitats of southwest Asia and north Africa. Often, they display a curious behavior that serves them well in these habitats - they skim over the surface of the water and then fly away quickly. This process does not give enough time for them to cool down, drink the water, or bathe in it. How does getting their belly wet help the survival of their species?

. . .

191. Along the steppes of Kalmykia in Eastern Europe, golden eagles often perch very close to the roads, unfrightened and unmoving despite the passing cars. What's more, the eagles have found a way to reap benefits from the vehicles that pass through their territory. Why do Kalmykia's golden eagles sit by the roadsides?

192. Child-rearing behavior across the natural world is incredibly diverse and fascinating. While studying the behavior of ostriches, ornithologists noted that once a few chicks appear in a clutch of eggs, the mother waits and watches for a while, and then breaks the unhatched eggs. Why would the mother destroy some eggs in each clutch?

HINTS:

189. *Nature can sometimes be paradoxical—animals living in deeper waters hunt by seeking brighter objects in darkness.*

190. *The birds are flying off on a critical mission beyond simply cooling themselves off.*

191. *While the passing cars may not frighten the golden eagles, perhaps they could frighten other steppe inhabitants?*

192. *The mother, they noted, was careful not to break eggs that had a chance of hatching. She does, however, break eggs that seem spoiled or unviable. What would happen once such bad eggs are broken?*

ANSWERS:

189A. By emitting a bright, light-colored liquid instead

Squids and octopuses living at greater, darker depths release bright blobs of liquid instead of their usual dark ink. These glowing clouds serve as decoys that deceive enemies into pursuing those instead of seeking out the cephalopod itself.

190A. To carry water droplets to their chicks.

Most species of sandgrouses seem to have highly evolved belly feathers that serve as sponges. During the breeding season, sand-grouses skim over the surface of water bodies, soak up water, and fly back to the nests. Their wet bellies help to both cool off the eggs on a hot day and hydrate the thirsty chicks.

191A. To catch scared prey in the wake of passing cars.

The steppes are inhabited by many kinds of rodents, like ground squirrels, jerboas, and others who spend their days well-hidden by the sparse steppe vegetation. When startled by cars, however, the rodents will run away from the roads, and into the patient talons of the hungry eagles.

192A. The smell of rotten, broken eggs attracts flies and other insects and provides the newly hatched chicks with fresh food.

In every clutch of birds' eggs, not every one is viable. After some chicks have hatched, the waiting period allows the mother to determine which eggs are likely spoiled and can be used to bait flies and insects instead. The successful chicks also start their life with a fresh, home-delivered meal.

193. When stealth technology was used for aircraft, it promised to make them 'invisible' to enemy radar. However, Colonel Barry Horn, one of the first to pilot stealth technology was skeptical. Yet one morning, he stumbled upon some animals in an F-117 plane hangar that made him change his mind. What do you think he stumbled upon?

194. Cuckoos are best-known for shirking their parental responsibilities and laying their eggs in other birds' nests. However, scientists studying this 'brood parasitism' behavior reported that crow nests with a cuckoo chick have better success against predators than nests without. What could explain this?

195. The breathtaking Yucatan Peninsula with its pristine turquoise lakes is the pride of Mexico. The landscape owes its beauty to the karst or limestone formations underground. To preserve this landscape, local authorities caution tourists wearing 'particular products' to not bathe in these lakes. What products are these?

HINTS:

193. *Stealth technology works by absorbing signals - who else emits signals similar to radar?*

194. *Could the cuckoo chicks be employing a more effective means to deter predators?*

195. *The locals fear that the products will not only pollute the water but also have an adverse effect on the limestone formations.*

ANSWERS:

193A. Bats.

Bats are practically blind and navigate via echolocation - they emit a series of ultrasound waves and listen for echoes to gauge distances between objects. Good stealth technology would work by absorbing or muffling ultrasound - either sonar or radar. That morning, Colonel Barry Horn found dead bats in the hangar and realized that the stealth crafts must have effectively dampened their ultrasound, and caused them to crash - and thereby, surmised that the stealth technology was really as effective as it claimed. Fun fact: experts later believed that the bats may have died rather due to the toxic paint used on the aircraft!

194A. Cuckoo chicks secrete a foul-smelling substance when they detect predators and are thereby able to protect their half-siblings.

The term 'brood parasitism' implies that one organism is thriving at the expense of another one. In the case of cuckoos, being louder in their demands, they secure more food, and thereby, are often stronger or even bigger than their half-siblings if their parents have chosen the nest of a smaller bird. In some cases, they outgrow the nest and the parents too. However, this ability to deter predators offers interesting insights into the relationship between cuckoo chicks and their foster families.

195A. Cosmetic products.

Karst or limestone landscapes are shaped by water eroding through the rock, forming a network of caves and subterranean waterways. The cosmetic products not only pollute the water but also cause further chemical weathering of the limestone.

196. In Israel, during the early flight tests of F-16 fighters, there were frequent failures of the computer navigation systems. It was observed that navigation often failed during flights over the Dead Sea. What could have caused such errors?

197. In Canada, the moose that wander through the tundra forests love eating the tender leaves, even though they are sometimes too high and out of reach. Yet they receive help from an unexpected quarter: a neighbor that they watch intently with the hope that they can reach some of the tender tundra foliage. Which wild neighbor do the moose have a relationship with to secure food?

HINTS:

196. *Apart from being the saltiest lake in the world, the Dead Sea is unique in another geographic parameter that confused the plane navigation systems. What is that?*

197. *The neighbor cannot help the moose reach greater heights, but perhaps, they can make the foliage from great heights reach the lower ground?*

ANSWERS:

196A. The low elevations around the Dead Sea caused the computer to classify its territory as underground or underwater. As these levels were below their specified parameters, the navigation devices malfunctioned.

The electronics used for flights in the 1960s were calibrated from 0 meters above sea level and were not prepared for the contingency that flights would fly below sea level. The Dead Sea lies at 430 meters below sea level, and even if the flights were flying a fair distance over it, they would still have been considered underwater or underground by the navigation systems.

197A. Beavers, who fell down tall trees as they build their dams across the waterways.

The rather unusual symbiosis between the moose and the beaver in Canada is among Nature's incredible relationships. The beavers not just fell tall trees and allow moose to access the tender leaves. Their dams also create little ponds that provide other essential nutrients for the moose.

THINK DIFFERENT

198. Stanford University is undeniably one of the best in the world. The following question was once proposed as a part of the qualifying exam for this prestigious university. You are expected to find a solution in 15 minutes using just what is provided to you: a box of matches and a piece of rope which you are informed takes precisely one hour to burn from end to end. However, the combustion rate may not be constant—it can burn quickly at first, then slow down, vice versa, or at any other varying speed. How do you measure 45 minutes just by setting fire to the rope?

HINTS:

198. *You are given precisely 15 minutes to come up with the solution.*

ANSWERS:

198A. Light one end of the rope as soon as the test time begins.

Remember how you were informed that it takes exactly 1 hour (or 60 minutes) for the rope to burn? By igniting the rope as soon as the test time begins, you'll know that the allotted 15 minutes will have passed once it is announced that your time is up. This would then mean the rope you are left with has 45 minutes of burning time to go.

QUESTIONS:

199. As a child, the famous speleologist Norbert Casteret loved to explore the caves near his house. He often returned home with chalky stains, much to his mother's chagrin. Young Norbert soon stumbled on an ingenious solution that allowed him to get home looking presentable and avoid punishment - what was it?

200. Any parent knows that the cycle of picking a baby's pacifier up off the floor and washing it only for it to be spit out or thrown again is such a hassle. One resourceful family came up with a solution to avoid this, using something that many children love. What is it?

201. A little boy once asked his father to buy him a new bicycle. As a compromise, his dad told him to sell lemonade, promising to give him the square of whatever amount he made in sales. The boy ended up selling $3 worth of lemonade. His father was happily willing to fork over the $9, only for his son to inform him that he actually owes much more! How could this be?

. . .

HINTS:

199. *He couldn't resist the chalky caves, and yet outwardly, he found a way to make it less obvious that he had been inside.*

200. *A thread was used to tie the pacifier to this object to prevent it from falling to the floor.*

201. *The math is correct. The little boy kept count of his earnings a little differently.*

ANSWERS:

199A. Young Norbert would turn his clothes inside out while exploring, and put them on the right way when he headed home.

The clothes were still dirty, but his appearance would not betray where he had been. We don't know how long this trick worked unless he was also laundering his own clothes afterward. But we do know that his childhood passion led to a career in cave exploration, and he even discovered prehistoric cave drawing at the Montespan caves in France.

200A. A balloon

They tied the pacifier to a floating, lighter-than-air helium balloon. That way, even if the baby spit it out or threw it, it would simply stay suspended in mid-air instead of falling on the dirty floor.

201A. By converting $3 into cents, the boy came to the grand total of $900.

$3 is equal to 300 cents, and the square of this is 90,000. Following the son's logic, his dad owed him $900!

❧ III ❦
EXTRA CHALLENGING
PROBLEMS

BUSINESS INNOVATIONS

202. In 1955, the first cigarette vending machines in the United States only accepted a minimal payment of 25 cents. However, some cigarettes were cheaper, and the vending machine was unable to dispense any smaller change. This frustrated buyers of cheaper cigarette brands, as they lost a few cents each time. Changing the size of the pack to a larger one with more cigarettes would be too problematic for different reasons; another innovative solution was needed. What solution did the manufacturers of the cigarette packets find to ensure customer satisfaction?

HINTS:

202. *The manufacturers started adding something to cigarette packets to help recoup the loss.*

ANSWERS:

202A. The manufacturers added a few cents to the cigarette packets, to make up for the difference between the cost and 25 cents.

As vending machines were a popular, easily accessible option to expand cigarette sales, the manufacturers decided to compensate the buyers by including the missing cents in the packets.

QUESTIONS:

203. Glenn Berger, a resident of Florida, became a millionaire by retrieving and reselling golf balls from locations that were otherwise difficult to get at. One of his hobbies made him especially adept at retrieving golf balls - which hobby could it be?

204. To boost company sales, entrepreneur Ari Weinzweig installed an object on every salesperson's desk in a way that made it easy to look at. What object could have helped win customers over and land more deals?

205. The government of Chile once struggled with systemic tax evasion. Because most shops and service centers took payment in cash, they intentionally avoided punching transactions in at the register and issuing receipts to the customers. In their efforts to counter this, the country's tax authority came up with an attractive incentive that had Chileans asking for all their receipts from businesses. What was this solution that officials came up with?

HINTS:

203. *The hobby involved getting balls from a rather difficult place, with the additional risk of running into alligators and snakes.*

204. *In the business world, they say, an upbeat salesperson lands more deals - what object would better remind employees to stay positive?*

205. *Just short of outright paying people to collect and submit their receipts—which the government couldn't possibly afford—how else could they give them an economic stake in this?*

ANSWERS:

203A. Diving.

Glenn amassed a fortune by tapping into his hobby. He dived with scuba gear to retrieve balls, which he would then sell to golf clubs.

204A. A table mirror.

Ari has consulted with psychologists, who had advised him that smiling more can help create a positive mood. He encouraged his employees to smile more often when talking to clients, and the table mirror was a reminder to smile and stay positive.

205A. Run a regular receipt lottery

Chilean tax authorities set up a lottery where receipts for every purchase and transaction were lottery tickets. Once residents had something to gain from collecting receipts, businesses were forced to regularly issue them, and of course, file and pay their corresponding taxes as a result. The increased tax collection was partially used to fund the lottery winnings—overall, a win-win for the state and its residents.

25

CULTURE & ARTS

206. The roots of using the term 'piracy' to refer to copyright infringement can be traced back to at least as early as 1603. In those days, it was common for rival theater companies and publishers to hunt down in-demand plays and take these for their own use. One such instance of intellectual property theft was Shakespeare's classic, "Hamlet." A year before publication by the official Shakespearean troupe, a pirated version of the play's text was released. Upon comparing editions of the text decades later, scholars were able to determine with near certainty that the thief was the actor who played Marcelo in the original Shakespearean troupe. How did they figure it out?

HINTS:

206. *The culprit was not careful in copying the text, so there were some inconsistencies between the original and pirated editions.*

ANSWERS:

206A. The character Marcelo's lines were true to Shakespeare's version —much of the other text differed significantly from the original.

It was easy to trace the piracy back to the actor who played the role. Because the actor knew his part by heart, he could reproduce this portion of the text perfectly. At the same time, all the other characters' lines were noticeably different from the original.

QUESTIONS:

207. It is said that the ancient Greek sculptor Phidias was commissioned for a statue of 'Athena the Virgin' and paid to use gold and ivory for his craft. To counter jealous detractors who might accuse him of stealing gold, the sculptor designed an ingenious way to use the precious metal in his statue. What unusual feature did his sculpture possess?

208. Typography design is an underappreciated art that involves designing fonts for use across mediums. The Times New Roman font is a popular choice for long-form writing. In September 2018, a US typography design agency designed a new font, that was a modification of the Times New Roman - its style was indistinguishable from the classic, yet each letter was expanded by 5-10%. What purpose could the updated font serve?

209. Paper currency is among the most powerful symbols of our time. When the American currency was being redesigned, the artists wanted to take the symbolism one step further: they hoped to depict that time would have no power over the dollar. What changes did the artists

incorporate to better symbolize the immortality of the dollar in the face of time?

HINTS:

207. *The parties who commissioned him, had exact accounts of how much gold was to be used for the sculpture. The gold parts of the statue were constructed in an unusual way that could help him establish veracity, and evade accusations of theft in the future.*

208. *With the updated font, written text can take up more volume. What written form would want a beefier, yet classic look?*

209. *American currency bears the faces of former presidents. The artists rendered a change on the faces of not just the banknotes but also that of the presidents.*

ANSWERS:

207A. The sculpture had detachable gold components that could be separated and weighed when required.

This anecdote is drawn from a time after Archimedes' bathtub experiment had yielded an accurate measure for weighing gold. If accused, Phidias could detach the gold components of the statue, weigh them, and reassure his clients that the amount of gold used was as intended.

208A. Student essays.

The Times New Roman font is most often seen in newsprints, where copious amounts of text are squeezed into panels. Most educational institutions insisted on using Times New Roman for student submissions. The revised Times New Roman font was targeted at school and college students who had to submit multi-page essays as assignments.

209A. They erased the wrinkles from the faces of former presidents.

Wrinkles are a visible sign of age or the power of time over people. The artists removed all traces of wrinkles from the faces that marked the American banknotes to ensure that the dollar could stake a claim as being more powerful than time.

26

FOLK WISDOM

210. The 18th century brought about the end of medieval times in the Alps, increasing cultural, societal, and technological advances. It was during this time that one Alpine castle maintained a single spear, stuck into its outdoor grounds. This spear was visited regularly by a castle guard, and during these routine checks, a halberd—a battle-ax with a long handle—would be touched to its metal tip. After this, the guard would sometimes ring a bell. When would the guard know to ring the bell?

HINTS:

210. *Ringing the bell was meant to warn others of potential danger and help them keep safe*

ANSWERS:

210A. When visible sparks jumped between the two metal objects

Globally, about 240,000 lightning-related accidents (some of which end up fatal) occur yearly, and high altitude areas such as the Alps are even more prone to these than lowlands. The spear and halberd system was an early way to help prevent these. If touching the halberd to the spear tip caused an electric charge to jump between the two, this meant that atmospheric conditions were just right for lightning. The castle guard would then ring the bell to warn everyone of the incoming thunderstorm.

QUESTIONS:

211. Medieval castles are distinguished by their architecture, and among the many features, a spiral staircase is often present. On most spiral staircases, those climbing would need to turn towards the right, and those descending would turn towards the left. What purpose did such spiral staircases serve?

212. The art of pearl diving was described in a book by Pliny, the ancient Roman historian. He noted that the sun's glare on the sea made it difficult for pearl divers to search for mollusk shells underwater - yet they were quick to innovate. What technique did the pearl divers employ to reduce the glare underwater?

213. In ancient Greece, rich hosts often held large feasts. To impress guests, they effected sudden changes in the scent of feast halls with the help of incense or perfume. Despite large halls, they were able to cause

changes in the smell of the room rapidly - what ingenious solution did they stumble upon?

HINTS:

211. *The spiral staircase is intended as a defense, and built on the premise that a majority of people are right-handed. How can the orientations of the ascending and descending parties help defend the castle better?*

212. *The technique involved carrying something underwater in their mouths which they could release at the bottom to cut down the glare at the surface. This ensured that their lungs could still hold in air and allowed their hands to be left free to collect mollusks.*

213. *There is a limit to how rapidly perfume or incense can diffuse through the air, but perhaps, the solution lies in natural dispersal? What method can be employed that would work faster than people carrying a scent across a room?*

ANSWERS:

211A. The spiral staircase would mean defenders from within would be in a better, more convenient position than the attackers, with greater room to move their right arms, and thereby, able to launch an offensive.

Most people tend to use weapons in their dominant hand, and thereby, more warriors would bear weapons in their right hands rather than the left. The spiral staircase would mean that the attacker going upstairs, would have his sword next to the wall on the right side; whereas the defender facing downstairs has enough open space to maneuver his sword.

212A. A slow release of olive oil at the bottom of the sea - where divers would seek mollusks.

Before going underwater, pearl divers would grab a lungful of air, a mouthful of olive oil, and slowly release the oil when they reached the bottom of the Mediterranean Sea. As oil is lighter than water, it would float to the surface creating a film that would reduce the glare, and allow the pearl divers to see more clearly and find the prized shells.

213A. Pigeons sprayed with perfume were released into the feast halls to ensure a quick dispersal of new fragrances.

As gradual diffusion could not be the solution, pigeons were sprayed with perfume and released to rapidly change scents across the feast halls. This method of natural dispersal was faster, and scented pigeons flying around the hallways would be more effective and impressive than if people were employed to do the same.

214. A Russian ethnographer once wrote about visiting a young Yakut couple in Siberia, where he noticed a moldering piece of wood in the house. Surprised, he asked the family what the wood was for. He learned that the wood was known as 'emyak', and was part of the Yakut tradition since ancient times. Before finding use in the house, the wood needed to be dried out well and cut into small pieces with a knife. After it has served its purpose, it is discarded. What possible purpose could the dried 'emyak' have served in the young couple's house?

215. In the olden days, it was common for some rural villages to have a certain length of the road layered thinly with tar, followed by a stretch sprinkled with dry sand. Who were then chased down such roads?

HINTS:

214. *Dry, moldering wood absorbs moisture well, and young Yakut couples tend to find a lot of use for 'emyak'. Modern couples today opt for a very different solution.*

215. *Stepping onto tar and then sand would result in a kind of protective shell.*

ANSWERS:

214A. The lining for a baby's bedsheet.

Dry, decaying wood is an excellent absorbent and can wick away moisture - almost like a sponge. The 'emyak' is used as a lining in the sheet of a baby's crib, to absorb the damp and keep the baby dry - especially useful in Siberia's cold climate, and as disposable diapers were not always available.

215A. Geese and similar flat-footed fowl

To create improvised "footwear" for geese, villagers had them first walk over sticky tar, which would then serve as the glue for the grains of sand in the next stretch of road. This protective gear enabled fowl to walk long distances without getting hurt, allowing villagers to drive them to market.

27

HISTORICAL HAPPENINGS

216. In the 19th Century, during the Franco-Prussian war, sending dispatches from Paris to the army on-ground was difficult - messengers were often intercepted by the Germans. The French started sending messages via pigeons instead, and the German rifles at the time weren't as effective in shooting them down. Eventually, the Germans found another method to interrupt the French messages - how do you think they did it?

HINTS:

216. *Instead of shooting pigeons, what other, more natural mechanism could be used to intercept messages on-the-wing?*

ANSWERS:

216A. The Germans released falcons to bring down the pigeons, and intercept the messages.

As falcons are natural predators of pigeons, releasing them to catch the flighted messengers proved more effective than shooting them down.

QUESTIONS:

217. The Roman commander, Decimus Junius Brutus, led many troops from the Lusitania to Galicia in order to conquer more territories. Yet when these bold warriors reached the banks of the River Lima they hesitated to traverse it, as the river bears a fearful myth. To dispel these fears, Brutus crossed the river and called out to each of his soldiers by name. What was the myth Brutus wished to prove wrong?

218. It is said that the commander Napoleon Bonaparte paid great attention to the appearance of his soldiers. His army was always stylishly outfitted, and their uniforms had beautiful pewter buttons. Yet, a particular situation led to a rather embarrassing wardrobe malfunction and forced his soldiers to hold up their pants to prevent them from falling. What could the problem be?

219. In 1806, two gentlemen, Humphrey Howarth and the Earl of Barrymore quarreled and challenged each other to a duel. As a former military surgeon, Howarth understood well how the dangers of a wound increased significantly if it was infected. How did Howarth prepare himself for the duel to minimize the risk of infection?

.   .   .

220. Innovations often have a cascading effect. In the 19th Century, during the Franco-Prussian War, when the French stumbled upon using pigeons to dispatch messages to their army - the Germans intercepted them by releasing falcons - natural predators of pigeons. The French found another way to bypass the falcons and ensure their pigeon-mail continued. What method do you think they employed?

HINTS:

217. *How could calling each soldier by name convince them that the myth was untrue and that they had nothing to fear?*

218. *The key lies in the pewter or tin buttons; what could have caused them to fail?*

219. *How do wounds get infected? Bullets are not the only way wounds can fester. Howarth's solution lay not in preparing himself with some-thing more, but with something less.*

220. *What if pigeons could scare off their predators? Is there any way we can 'equip' them to do so?*

ANSWERS:

217A. The myth claimed that crossing the Lima river would cause memory loss.

Believing the river Lima caused forgetfulness, none of the men wanted to run the risk of forgetting their past life, their family, or their homeland. By crossing the river and calling out to each of his soldiers by name, the commander convinced them that his memory was still intact and the myth was untrue.

218A. Fighting battles in the extreme cold of Russia caused the pewter buttons to turn to white powder!

Napoleon's army fought in many different weather conditions and yet managed to look sharp. Yet when they fought in Russia during the winter, the pewter buttons - mainly consisting of tin, cracked and turned to powder. This is known as a "tin pest", and soldiers were forced to hold up their pants. What a sight it must have been!

219A. Howarth came to the duel naked.

Threads from clothing find their way into a wound, causing it to be infected further and fester. To counter this, Howarth appeared at the duel completely naked. If you are curious, his opponent was so shocked, he refused to fight Howarth - it looks like his strategy paid off better than he'd imagined. No wound, no infection!

220A. Pigeons with whistles attached to their tail

Falcons are wary of sharp sounds. Attaching small whistles to the tails of pigeons, which emitted a sharp sound while in flight due to the rushing air, seemed to deter the falcons and allowed the pigeons to deliver their messages unharmed, and in time.

221. The 1947 Kon-Tiki expedition was an ambitious raft journey across the Pacific Ocean from South America to the Polynesian Islands. While carrying out their mission, Kon-Tiki's crew ran into a certain problem, which they radioed to the coast. Experts from Los Angeles then informed them that the heat was to blame. To combat this, the crew used a vessel of carbon dioxide to create dry ice. What did they cool with this ice?

222. Before the famous Battle of Austerlitz, Napoleon's troops were stationed at Pratzen Heights - a gently sloping hill that was a good vantage point for the French army. However, one cloudy morning in November 1805, Napoleon noticed something that could offer him a decisive advantage and had his troops descend from the high ground to assume positions in the valley below. The enemy troops assumed this was a mistake and marched up to the high ground - yet this proved to be one of Napoleon's most astute, and shrewd battle decisions. This battle is among the greatest victories under Napoleon, and the French troops went on the offensive to win against the larger Russian and Austrian armies. What did this strategy rely on that made it difficult for the Russian and Austrian armies on high ground to win against the French troops below?

HINTS:

221. *Documentation and filming were key elements on the Kon-Tiki voyage.*

222. *Note, the day was cloudy and humid yet it did not rain. What weather phenomenon could have turned the advantage of higher terrain around on its head, and allowed Napoleon to catch the enemy by surprise?*

ANSWERS:

221A. Film developer liquid, fixer, and other solutions used for photography

Upon processing the first few strips of film onboard, crew members of the Kon-Tiki discovered that these were damaged. When developing film, it is crucial to keep all solutions under 16°C — quite a challenging feat on a raft in the middle of the sea! The Hollywood experts Kon-Tiki's crew got in touch with came up with the suggestion to use dry ice, allowing them to cool the solutions without diluting or otherwise affecting these chemicals' potency.

222A. Fog.

The cloudy November day was marked by fog, which tends to settle in valleys. On that day, Napoleon abandoned the high ground to lead his troops into the cover of the fog, was able to take the enemy troops by surprise, and launch offensive attacks from different, unexpected directions. The Battle of Austerlitz was among the most decisive engagements in the Napoleonic Wars.

❄ 28 ❄

HOW'D THEY DO IT?

223. To make a perfect cup of Norwegian coffee, you need 3 ingredients: freshly brewed coffee decoction, whisky, and a coin. The process involves placing the coin at the bottom of the cup, adding the decoction, and then the whisky. How can you ensure a perfect brew?

HINTS:

223. *What role could the coin at the bottom of the cup play in this strange process? It has to do with being able to see the coin.*

ANSWERS:

223A. First, the dark decoction poured over the coin hides it from view. Next, topping it up with whisky, one pours till the coin is visible again - and voila, you have the perfect Norwegian coffee!

The coin ensures the correct proportions between the coffee decoction and the whisky.

HUMAN BEHAVIOR

224. In the 1970s, the Italian company Fiat decided to modernize and install robots on their assembly lines. The company decided to use people as prototypes to optimize the robots' performance and ensure they don't spend energy on unnecessary movements. Company representatives were sent out to recruit these 'prototypes,' who were offered a good fee to work on the assembly lines for a short period of time and were closely watched. What skills in these 'prototype people' was the company interested in, that would inspire their robots?

HINTS:

224. *The company was eager to optimize the energy usage and thereby minimize unnecessary movement on the part of the robots. What kind of people will optimize for such actions to ensure they don't tire out?*

ANSWERS:

224A. Laziness - the company recruited self-proclaimed lazy people who did not use unnecessary movements to get the work done.

The company's scientists decided that lazy people would serve as prototypes for their assembly line robots as they optimize for movements. By watching how the 'prototype people' operated, the scientists were able to design their robots to be just as economical with their motion and yet efficient at getting the work done.

QUESTIONS:

225. So many innovative ideas have been rolled out to make life easier for astronauts in a spacesuit. A mirror on the wrist helps them read the numbers of the instruments on their chests. A tube is installed under the helmet to allow for drinking. Interestingly, in the early 1970s, astronauts requested a small pad be attached to the inside of their helmets, midway down the face visor. This request wasn't for any vital function, nor to do with their work on the spaceship. What possible use could this pad serve?

226. To err is human, to not admit one's errors is more so, as American behavioral researchers studied in the last century. In an experiment, they left 25 cents in a phone booth. When someone entered and used it for their call, one of the researchers would pretend to have forgotten the money and would return with a smile and ask if it had been discovered. More than half the respondents lied. The researchers then changed something in the experiment, resulting in a seventy percent decrease in the number of liars. What did they change?

.   .   .

227. Heinrich Schliemann was a German adventurer and multimillionaire who went down in history as the man who discovered the buried remains of ancient Troy. Aside from his archaeological pursuits, Schliemann was also famous for his eccentricity. One such incident of his peculiar behavior almost caused a scandal at his son's baptism. While actually quite logical, what he did enraged the priest, who then had to be persuaded by Heinrich's wife to reconsecrate the water in the font. What did Schliemann do that caused such an uproar?

HINTS:

225. *What problem seems trivial to you, and is easily resolved by the use of your hands, that astronauts inside a spacesuit might find tricky, and would use the small pad for instead?*

226. *How would you break the ice with strangers and ensure that they feel warmer towards you?*

227. *Like any good father, Schliemann was just concerned for his child's health and wellbeing.*

ANSWERS:

225A. To scratch their noses!

Surely we all know that moment when our hands have been busy or full, and our nose needs a little scratch? Now imagine astronauts stuck inside spacesuits, repairing some part of their ship on the spacewalk, unable to get at that itch through their visors. The pad inside the helmet was perfect for helping them scratch their noses and then continue their work.

226A. They added a handshake to the experiment.

In the first scenario, the researchers tried to establish a connection with a smile and a request. However, they found that a handshake was more likely to establish a rapport and ensure that the strangers in the booth returned the money.

227A. He put a thermometer into the already-consecrated water.

Right before his son was dipped into the baptismal font, Schliemann produced a thermometer from his pocket and dipped it into the consecrated water, ensuring it was at an optimal temperature for the baby.

I WONDER WHY...?

228. Stockholm City Hall houses one of the city's most famous tourist sites: the Blue Hall. This ceremonial hall is known for being the venue for the annual Nobel Banquet, a grand dinner for the year's laureates. Perhaps the most prominent feature of the Blue Hall is its marble staircase, down which each person of honor descends at the beginning of the prestigious celebration. To help certain professionals who often worked at such events, Ragnar Östberg, the architect of the City Hall, requested for a star to be placed on the wall opposite these stairs. Why?

HINTS:

228. *Thanks to this star, photographers and videographers can take great shots. How does it help?*

ANSWERS:

228A. The star naturally draws the eye, positioning the guests' heads at an optimal angle as they descend the stairs.

Don't you often find yourself looking down at your feet when you make your way down flights of stairs? Well, if the Nobel Banquet's guests were to do the same, it would result in unflattering photos and videos. The star on the opposite wall provides a natural focal point up ahead to gaze at, allowing for photographers to take beautiful, dignified shots of the laureates as they enter the ceremonial hall.

QUESTIONS:

229. In the Middle Ages, publishers were in the habit of adding non-existent locations like islands, rivers, or towns to geographical maps and atlases. The places themselves were rather minor, unimportant, and would not have been used by anyone. What purpose could such additions serve the publisher?

230. In the heart of Amsterdam, old quarters have narrow two or three-storied houses along each side of the street. Oddly, there's a big hook located near the wide window of every floor in the building - what purpose could these hooks serve?

231. In an experimental program rolled out in several US prisons, gun shooting ranges are set up for inmates' use. What is the aim of this initiative?

. . .

232. At the start of the 20th century, engineers at a machinery factory in Russia were faced with one technical problem. To solve it, they turned to the local cathedral, more specifically, the choir leader. What service could the choir leader have rendered to the factory engineers?

HINTS:

229. *These details were added just like other, real, place names on the map. What could be the function of such false information printed on maps?*

230. *The buildings in these parts of Amsterdam also have rather narrow flights of stairs. How could hooks offset the inconvenience of narrow stairwells?*

231. *The guiding principle behind it is that in theory, improving criminals' shooting accuracy will actually help improve the safety of law-abiding citizens.*

232. *The factory was responsible for the assembly of steam locomotives. How could the choir leader get the engineers back on track?*

ANSWERS:

229A. To protect copyright and avoid plagiarism.

The Middle Ages were marked by leaps in navigation, both on land and at sea. Maps were crucial to navigators, and plotting locations was a well-guarded art. Only publishers knew which placenames were fictitious, and a copied map would blindly have copied all details. Adding false information helped publishers prove ownership, avoid counterfeiting, and sue others for intellectual property infringements.

230A. To lift furniture or bulky household items into the apartments.

Real estate in Amsterdam has always been expensive, and the old quarters were built in a somewhat economical style. The narrow flights of stairs pose an inconvenience to moving any bulky household items. The hooks allow a rope to be tied, and the furniture and other items to be lifted into the apartments and carried in through the wide windows.

231A. To reduce the number of unintended collateral damage during gang gunfights

While ideally, prison inmates would never return to a life of crime even once released, the reality is that this may not always be the case. The goal of this highly controversial experiment is to prepare for the worst. Should criminals find themselves in a street gunfight again, it would perhaps be the lesser evil for them to be able to accurately target each other rather than accidentally shoot passers-by.

232A. Tuning the whistle of the steam locomotive.

As per the legal standards, steam locomotive whistles had to have a specific tonality based on their type and purpose. Tuning the whistles needed a 'perfect musical ear,' and the engineers had turned to the choir leader to help them adjust the whistle.

INGENIOUS INVENTIONS

233. One day, in 1884, Chicago engineer William Jenny's wife was cleaning their bookshelves when she accidentally knocked over a thick, heavy volume, dropping it on top of a birdcage on the floor. Upon seeing that the cage was completely undamaged, Jenny came to an ingenious solution to an issue he had been grappling with at work—a problem so challenging that it kept him from accepting a certain job. After witnessing his wife's incident with the birdcage, he then decided to take the project on, producing the first of its kind in 1885. What was it?

HINTS:

233. *Jenny realized that a structure made of thin metal wires—much like the birdcage—could be both durable and lightweight. He then applied this concept to a Chicago construction project.*

ANSWERS:

233A. The first skyscraper

During those days, construction was mainly done with large masses of brick and concrete, which came with the issue of too much weight and instability the higher a structure got. Inspired by how the birdcage withstood force, Jenny came up with the technology of using light and firm steel skeletons for buildings. Using this technology, the first 10-story, 42-meter high skyscraper was built in Chicago in 1885.

QUESTIONS:

234. In foundries, metal was often cleaned by sandblasting. However, sand tends to clog up the cavities in intricate metal parts. Water makes for a poor cleaning solution as it causes rust. Cleaning liquids aren't much help either for the more resistant, resiny clogs. Michael Michalko realized another substance could work as an abrasive cleaner and be easier to clean than sand - what alternative did he suggest?

235. Have you ever wondered how ships are launched into the water from land? These vessels are usually gradually slid down a ramp or slipway to ensure a soft launch into the water. Typically, various lubrication is used to aid this process: oils, waxes, and other synthetic substances. However, these lubricants are often water pollutants. In India, they could devise an easy, natural substitute to help remedy this. What is this, that they used to soften ships' descent into the water?

236. Sometimes, extraordinary ideas come at the most ordinary moments. Amateur rocket science enthusiast Derek Willis came up with an idea for rocket fuel innovation during a snack break. Willis

invented a safer solid rocket fuel that doesn't require the injection of an oxidizing agent during combustion. What was he snacking on when this idea occurred to him?

237. Sharks are one of the oceans' deadliest predators, known to attack other sealife and humans alike. In the 20th century, American engineer Johnson proposed a new way to protect humans from sharks. For this, he used learnings from an experiment with tuna, in which the fish were placed in a pool and deliberately frightened with blows to the water. Water from this pool was then transferred to another pool with peacefully swimming sharks... which then became agitated and began to search aggressively for prey. Based on this observation, what kind of protection for humans was proposed?

HINTS:

234. *Can a substance act as sand while cleaning clogged cavities and yet clean itself up with no effort, literally disappearing after a short time?*

235. *They used a plant byproduct abundant in the country, making this alternative not just eco-friendly but also incredibly cheap.*

236. *The core concept of the solid fuel was to contain oxygen in a 'bound' form within solid fuel.*

237. *The tuna apparently released some kind of substance into the water, attracting sharks.*

ANSWERS:

234A. Dry Ice.

Dry ice or frozen, solidified carbon dioxide is a great agent to clean metal when it emerges from the foundry with traces of residual material. It acts as solid sand to cleanse the metal, skips the liquid stage in a process known as sublimation, and dissolves in the air to form gaseous carbon dioxide (CO_2). Today, it is widely used across metal foundries for no-fuss, no-muss cleaning.

235A. Banana peels

Industrial synthetic lubricants, specialized oils, and even moving streams of air or bubbles are all used for lowering ships along slipways and into the water. As a much more cost-effective and environmentally-friendly alternative, India started using slippery banana peels instead.

236A. A porous chocolate bar

Willis was inspired by the unique texture of one of his favorite treats, a snack bar with dozens of tiny bubbles made by aerating chocolate. He came up with the idea that solid fuel could be made in a similar way, trapping bubbles of oxygen necessary for the combustion process.

237A. Waterproof diving suit

Assuming that the human body also secretes similar substances that sharks could detect and were attracted to, Johnson suggested using waterproof suits to prevent these from being released into the water.

❧ 32 ❧

NATURE & SCIENCE

238. There is a technique in science that relies on cultivating bacteria on agar, and providing it with specific nutrients and human secretions, to help decipher certain clues. If the nutrients and secretions are laid out in a particular pattern, bacterial colonies tend to mimic that pattern. Therefore, scientists can use it, encouraging the bacteria to grow where certain human secretions have been deposited. What clues can such bacterial patterns reveal?

HINTS:

238. *The nutrients, in this case, come from human cells or sebum, an oily secretion from human skin, which forms different patterns. Why would scientists wish to recreate these via bacterial colonies?*

ANSWERS:

238A. Indistinct or impartial fingerprints.

As the bacterial patterns mimic the patterns left behind by human cells or sebum, it is possible to recreate human fingerprints. Bacteria can amplify the weakest traces that might be difficult to find by other methods, and make fingerprints much easier to identify. Forensic scientists have been using this technique to recreate, identify and document indistinct or impartial fingerprints from crime scenes.

QUESTIONS:

239. At the beginning of the 19th century, doctor Francisco de Balmis embarked on a journey from Spain to the New World, taking several boys from a local orphanage with him. Historically, this trip is widely considered the first international medical expedition. Why did the doctor take these children on this voyage?

240. For 45 years, George Aldrich has been among NASA's important experts. Aldrich does not work with either technology, nor is he an astronaut, yet no item is carried onto a spacecraft without his examination. This examination is crucial in avoiding both physical and emotional discomfort to astronauts. What is Aldrich's specific function?

241. Woodcocks are long-billed, wading birds, best known for their funny 'bobbing' way of walking. Naturalists have noted that the woodcock hunts for food by stomping and knocking lightly over the ground, thereby deceiving its prey. How does the woodcock's odd behavior deceive its prey?

. . .

HINTS:

239. *During this time, a widespread infectious disease plagued America. Apparently, Dr. de Balmis' mission on his trip was to help.*

240. *How can objects, especially personal items cause physical and emotional discomfort in a closed space?*

241. *The woodcock's thin, long bill is adapted for hard-to-reach places. A light knocking acts as deception by mimicking a particular natural phenomenon - for what underground prey could such a deception work?*

ANSWERS:

239A. As carriers of the smallpox vaccine

Even today, many vaccines use live derivatives of one form or another of the illnesses they are intended to target. Vaccines of the early 19th century were no different... except back then, there were no refrigerators to prolong the shelf-life of these 'live' substances. So, Dr. de Balmis used these children as living 'containers' to transport the vaccine and preserve its freshness. This method successfully stopped and prevented the further spread of smallpox, first in Mexico and Latin America, then with a new team of boys, the Philippines and China.

240A. Aldrich was in charge of odor testing, meaning he smelled all the items destined for space.

Due to the vacuum in space, there is no ventilation on spacecraft. An unpleasant smell will persist with no way to be rid of it. Aldrich's sensitive olfaction ensures astronauts have a comfortable haul in closed spacecraft. His formal job title is "chemical specialist".

241A. The woodcock's light tapping mimics the rhythm of the rain, and earthworms below the surface are tricked into crawling out, thereby securing a juicy snack for the bird.

In addition to this, the woodcock also rocks its body back and forth on damp ground, causing the worms to squirm underfoot. This makes them easier to detect, and the woodcock can poke a hole with its long bill and grab any earthworms hidden underground.

WHAT'S NEXT?

I hope this book gave you and perhaps your friends and family an enriching, enjoyable, and challenging experience! If you liked this book, I'd love to hear all about it — please do leave a review on Amazon and any socials. Here is the direct link:

http://review241.inventanddiscover.com

I take great care in ensuring the books' accuracy and overall quality, and I always stay open to suggestions. Should you spot any issues or have any thoughts on what I can do better, please don't hesitate to reach out via email or the official Facebook page.

Finally, keep an eye out for more coming up in this series! Be the first to know — join the mailing list and Facebook group to get exclusive access to fun freebies and promos on all the exciting new books we've got in store.

www.inventanddiscover.com

facebook.com/inventanddiscover
amazon.com/author/inventanddiscover
goodreads.com/inventanddiscover
bookbub.com/authors/invent-and-discover

BONUS - DON'T FORGET YOUR FREE EBOOKS.

Included with the purchase of this book are:

- More brain-teaser problems, with media materials. Download an illustrated ebook.
- SCAMPER - Techniques and tips for developing brainstorm-thinking strategy. How to use problems from this book for training. Download an ebook.
- Access to members-only content and offers via our social groups

Have your FREE copies sent to your inbox:

http://bonus.inventanddiscover.com

Made in the USA
Monee, IL
06 February 2022

90738249R00125